JESUS IS THE WORD

How to approach the Bible as Jesus Himself and receive
a personalized redemptive message from heaven for a free
purposeful victorious life on earth

Kenneth Sippola

ISBN 979-8-88685-950-8 (paperback)
ISBN 979-8-88685-951-5 (digital)

Christian Faith Publishing
832 Park Avenue
Meadville, PA 16335
www.christianfaithpublishing.com

Printed in the United States of America

CONTENTS

ACKNOWLEDGEMENTS

Pastor David Oberg—My father in the faith and who Pastored me and taught me what I know

Pastor Jerry Marino—The Prophet of God who became my burning bush and lit a fire in me to get this book going

Reena Sippola—My precious bride who encouraged and supported me throughout this entire process

INTRODUCTION

The Word of God is like no other. It's more than just a book; it's a book full of life. The Word is life-changing, and anyone who reads it is impacted forever. Many simply refer to it as the Bible, which it is, but there are many bibles in the world. But...there is only one Word of God.

When the authors of the Bible penned the Word of God, I wonder how many actually knew what it would become. Some, like Luke, just wrote because it "seemed right to do so." Just seeming right to do so doesn't sound to me like he knew this was going to be a letter placed among the other pages that comprise the most important book in all of history.

When we approach the Word correctly, we get so much more than we bargained for. In this book, I am going to highlight how to approach the Word of God and receive more from Him in your Word study time. There will be some Greek, Hebrew, and ancient Hebrew words within these pages, but don't feel like you have to be a linguist in order to understand the Word of God. However, the words within the Bible were not originally English, surprise, surprise. Hebrew and Aramaic were the original language in the Old Testament. Greek was used in the New Testament which then was translated into English.

I view the Word of God as a big love letter. The lover of my soul wrote me a letter to tell me how much He loves me. However, He speaks another language. Some people helped me and translated the letter into my language so I can read what He wrote. However, English can lack in explanation with just words. English requires emotion. For example, and an example many are already so familiar with, *love*. In English, if I say I love you to a friend and I say I love you to my wife, to the hearer, assuming they don't know me or know who I am talking to, I love both of these people the same. They have no idea what manner of love I have for these two people except for the plain fact that I said I love you.

Now, if the hearer knew the people I was talking to, they would assume that I love you means more to my wife than to a friend. In the Greek, there are different kinds of love that can be explained with just the word itself. I can say I love you to a friend in Greek, and a Greek hearer could more accurately assume that I was talking to a friend by the word love that was used. Likewise, if I were to say I love you to my wife in Greek, then the hearer could more accurately assume that I was talking to my wife just by hearing the word love in Greek. There is only one love in English, but what manner of love is defined by who is talking to whom and the emotion that is involved with the saying I love you. In Greek, all that is needed is the word only. There are four Greek words for love:

> ἀγάπη (Agape) = Unconditional love. True love.
> The deepest kind of love.
> Ἔρως (Eros) = Passionate love. A love with sensual desire and longing.
> φιλία (Philia) = Friendship and affectionate love. A general love between friends and family.
> στοργή (Storge) = Affection. Acceptance with putting up with situations.

If my wife only knew Greek and she wrote a love letter to me in Greek, then I would need someone to translate it for me so I knew what she said. If the translator only translated the word with no expression or definition, then where my wife would say, "Agape," the translator would translate simply, "I love you." In another area, she says, "Philia;" again, the translator would translate, "I love you." I would read the letter as her saying that she loves me and that was it, assuming that there was no other explanations, but if I did some research and found out that in one area of her letter, she actually said that she loves me unconditionally, and then in another area, she said that she really loved me as a friend or a brother, I can start to see what she was actually saying to me, and I can connect with her letter to me in a better way.

Likewise, with the Word of God, there was an original language that was spoken and translated before it came to English. Even when it did come to English, there are some words that lack the expression of what I believe the Father was truly communicating to us. We come to agree with what He said but so limited in agreement because we don't understand the complete meaning of what He was saying. Don't misunderstand me. Just because we don't speak Hebrew or Greek doesn't mean we haven't truly come to agree with what God is saying. He knows our hearts… What I am saying is there's much more for us to understand! It doesn't affect the way He looks at us and receives us, but it will affect the way we look at Him and receive Him. When we get a better understanding of what's really being said, we will receive more, know more, and experience a greater impact from the Word of God.

The Greek is expressive; the Hebrew has unlimited meaning, and the ancient Hebrew continues within that unlimited meaning. The ancient Hebrew is ancient and goes all the way back to when people would write the images in rocks to communicate to each other. I believe your faith will increase as you see Jesus even in the ancient letters thousands of years before His walk on the earth.

You do not have to become a linguist to understand the Word of God. All I am introducing is some depth to your understanding to reveal Jesus to you in a deeper way through the interpretation of the ancient Hebrew, the Hebrew, and the Greek. May you see Jesus as the Word and more after reading these pages, and may you receive more of His love for you which is unlimited in its giving.

CHAPTER 1

Words

Words are powerful. Words can create war and peace. Words can make friends and enemies. Words create and destroy. There's a tremendous amount of power in words. But how does that work? How can a mouth soothe rage and yet from the same mouth create rage? James says it well in James 3:3–8:

> Behold, we put bits in the horses' mouths, that they may obey us; and we turn about their whole body. Behold also the ships, which though *they be* so great, and *are* driven of fierce winds, yet are they turned about with a very small helm, whithersoever the governor listeth. Even so the tongue is a little member, and boasteth great things. Behold, how great a matter a little fire kindleth! And the tongue *is* a fire, a world of iniquity: so is the tongue among our members, that it defileth the whole body, and setteth on fire the course of nature; and it is set on fire of hell. For every kind of beasts, and of birds, and of serpents, and of things in the sea, is tamed, and hath been tamed of mankind: But the tongue can no man tame; *it is* an unruly evil, full of deadly poison.

The word *tongue* that is used in these verses is the Greek word γλῶσσα (glōssa) which means "the tongue, a member of the body, an organ of speech, the language or dialect used by a particular people distinct from that of other nations." This word could mean the actual tongue that is in the mouth or it could mean language. In this case, it is talking about the tongue in terms of language. Consider how powerful language is with God's words and actions at the tower of Babel.

> And the whole earth was of one language, and of one speech. And it came to pass, as they journeyed from the east, that they found a plain in the land of Shinar; and they dwelt there. And they said one to another, Go to, let us make brick, and burn them thoroughly. And they had brick for stone, and slime had they for morter. And they said, Go to, let us build us a city and a tower, whose top *may reach* unto heaven; and let us make us a name, lest we be scattered abroad upon the face of the whole earth. And the LORD came down to see the city and the tower, which the children of men builded. And the LORD said, Behold, the people *is* one, and they have all one language; and this they begin to do: and now nothing will be restrained from them, which they have imagined to do. Go to, let us go down, and there confound their language, that they may not understand one another's speech. So the LORD scattered them abroad from thence upon the face of all the earth: and they left off to build the city. Therefore is the name of it called Babel; because the LORD did there confound the language of all the earth: and from thence did the LORD scatter them abroad upon the face of all the earth. (Genesis 11:1–9)

The whole earth was of one speech, and now, nothing will be restrained from them which they have imagined to do. They had evil imaginations, and it was coming out of their mouths. They were all on the same page together, and whatever evil they saw within themselves to do, they were going to do, and they could have done it. But God intervened. He separated their language because they were about to destroy themselves.

The thing that I wanted to point out in this is the power of words. These people, at this time, moved God, whether good or bad; their one language caused God to move and intervene with their plans. The Creator of all things visible and invisible was moved at their speech.

> For *with the heart* man believeth unto righteousness; and *with the mouth* confession is made unto salvation. (<u>Romans 10:10</u>)

Words are not randomly formed when people are talking. Words are created with purpose and come from what's within. Notice here in Romans 10:10: "For *with the heart man believeth…and with the mouth confession…*" Words expose how we are feeling about something and our internal intents. The heart believes, and the mouth confesses that belief. The mouth reveals what's in the heart. If the word of our mouth can determine our eternal destiny, I would consider that to be some power!

God said in Genesis 11 with the Tower of Babel, "Nothing will be restrained from them, which they have imagined to do." The reason nothing would be held back from them is because they were all unified in speech. However, it all began in the imagination. Speech, or words, come from the heart or the place of the imagination. The heart is the seat of the *mind*, will, and emotions. Therefore, the imaginations would spring from this place of the heart.

Some would say that they don't say everything that's in their heart. Some actually speak contrary to what's inside. Now this could be good, or it could be bad. For instance, if one knows something to be the truth, and the truth is not what comes from the mouth but another thing, that would be called a lie. However, if something comes up on the inside of a person, say anger or sudden wrath, and this person decides not to say what's on the inside because it doesn't actually agree with the Word or who they are or what they actually feel about the person or situation, then that would be a good thing. The beauty of it all is that we have the power to choose what we want to connect with and let out of our mouths. We have the opportunity to discern what we let out of our mouths.

Continuing to examine Romans 10:10, let's look at the word *mouth* which is the Greek word στόμα (stoma) and it means, "the mouth, as part of the body, an opening." This is where we get our word *stomach*, stoma-ch. We know the stomach to be the place where our food digests, but this word also means midriff and belly. This happens to be where our spirit-man resides. We are, after all, a three-part being: spirit, soul, and body. The spirit does not reside in the digestive tract but in the belly, the midriff.

We know the lungs fill with air when we breathe, but it's not only the lungs that are involved; it's our bellies that play a part as well. I'm not a doctor or a physiologist, but I do know how to read, and from what I have come to know is right below the lungs, we have a diaphragm. This muscle contracts when we breathe, and it helps bring the air in, like a vacuum, and push the air right back out. That's the natural function of our "belly" breathing. However, I find it to be worth some more consideration on the spiritual end as the belly is where the Spirit resides.

Our vocal abilities are designed to speak the words of our spirit—hence, "stoma-ch." Yes, the mouth leads to the stomach, but there's more to the belly, or the midriff, than just digesting food. We have come to speak other words which we have learned along the way, but that was not the original intention. What happened in the garden of Eden with what we've come to know as the "original sin" is a double mind entered into man. The original construct of man was as it is today: spirit, soul, and body, but there was one mind. They still had the ability to choose just as we do, but the way they would think about God and life was all single-mindedness. When man chose to follow the other voice, another mind entered in which is called the mind of the flesh. It is talked about in the Book of Galatians in some more detail to understand the contrasts between the mind of the spirit and the mind of the flesh (Galatians 5:16–26).

Words are breath, or spirit, clothed in physical elements in order for the hearer to understand what is being said. You breathe out normally, and your thoughts are not known. If you breathe out heavily, it may cause someone to ask what's wrong? Why? Because the breathing pattern changed. But when we take that breath, and we clothe them in physical matter called words, then we don't have to just make breathing noises to get attention; we can say something that will communicate the need, or our thoughts, to others or to things.

> For verily I say unto you, That *whosoever shall say* unto this mountain, Be thou removed, and be thou cast into the sea; and *shall not doubt in his heart*, but shall believe that those *things which he saith* shall come to pass; he shall have *whatsoever he saith*. (Mark 11:23)

> Of the *abundance of the heart* his *mouth speaketh*. (Luke 6:45)

Our words, however finite in holding, are infinite in effect. Our words have the power to move mountains! They have the power to move people! I think people can be harder to move than mountains sometimes. They have the power to heal and to save.

See where the actual power comes from. It's not really in the word alone but what is inside that word that was spoken. Words are containers that carry the intent, or the seed, of its progenitor. This is why some music lyrics are not good to listen to. There are some preachers that are not good to listen to either. Those words are seeds that will produce something in the hearer. That something will either be life or death. The mouth forms the physical matter of words to clothe the thoughts from the abundance of the heart. The word abundance in the Greek is περίσσευμα (perisseuma) which means "in which one delights, of that which fills the heart, that which is left over, residue, remains, a surplus, or superabundance."

What is thought about most of the time is what is going to come out of the mouth, and that is the way one's life will go. It is what has been thought about over and over and over again or even heard through some other influence over and over and over again until it flows out of the mouth. "Sticks and stones may break my bones but words will never hurt me." Somebody else's words may not hurt you, but if you keep listening to damaging words, it sure can and will. However, your own words is where the greatest effect lies, and it will either do you good or bad.

It all starts with what's inside. Those words that are spoken are filled with something. It's not just some air; it's actually filled with meaning and purpose that even has the ability to move mountains. But it all starts in the mind. This is why it so critical that we renew our minds to the Word of God.

> And be not conformed to this world: but be
> ye transformed by the *renewing of your mind*, that
> ye may prove what *is* that good, and acceptable,
> and perfect, will of God. (<u>Romans 12:2</u>)

The word *renewing* in the Greek is ἀνακαίνωσις (anakainōsis) which means "a renewal, renovation, complete change for the better." We are instructed to make the complete change for the better in our minds. This word comes from ἀνακαινόω (anakainoō) and this means "to cause to grow up, new, to make new, new strength and vigor is given to one, to be changed into a new kind of life as opposed to the former corrupt state." This renewal of mind is not just for the unbelievers to become believers; this is also for the believers to grow up! There's a need to grow up spiritually in our walk with the Lord. It is only through our continual renewal of the mind that we can grow up and be the mature children of God that He wants us to become. Is there a weakness somewhere in you? Some place that you're struggling in your faith toward God? *Renew* your mind! He will give you new strength and vigor to accomplish anything He has set in your heart to do!

Let's look at Romans 10:10 again…"For with the heart man believeth unto righteousness; and with the mouth *confession* is made unto salvation."

The heart believes first unto righteousness and the mouth makes the confession. The word *confession* in the Greek is ὁμολογέω (homologeō) means "to say the same thing as another (i.e., to agree with, assent, to profess, to declare openly, speak out freely)"—the mouth coming in agreement with the heart. This is why it's so important that we renew our minds to the Word of God so we can come in agreement with His ways, plans, and purposes. So when we have our minds renewed, we make His Word our word. We fill our words with His breath releasing them into the earth and into people.

> It is the spirit that quickeneth; the flesh
> profiteth nothing: the words that I speak unto
> you, *they* are spirit, and *they* are life. (John 6:63)

Every word of the Word of God contains the breath of God. When we listen to or read His word, it is Him breathing His very nature and character into us. The word *spirit* literally means breath. In every word and every letter of the Word of God contains every bit of the Lord. It contains His presence, His essence, His power and glory. When the fivefold gifts are in operation proclaiming the Word of God, they are unpacking this breath and releasing it into people and into the atmosphere.

Words are like capsules. The capsule itself is just the transportation for the real thing to get to its destination—the real thing being the contents inside the capsule. Consider Proverbs 23:6–7: "Eat thou not the bread of *him that hath* an evil eye, neither desire thou his dainty meats: For as he thinketh in his heart, so *is* he: Eat and drink, saith he to thee; but his heart *is* not with thee." Although he saying go ahead and enjoy yourself, he really wishes that the person he is feeding doesn't eat too much because he's really the counting the cost of it all. The real contents of what he is saying is inside the word not so much the word itself. As he thinks in his heart so is he. That is true to all of us. What we think about most of the time is the way we will go and become. We must renew our minds to the Word of God.

If our words contain tremendous amount of power, how much more God's? Think about your own words and what you've been able to do just with your words alone. If you're married, it's because you asked or were asked. You made friends because of your words, and you've made enemies because of your words. When you can change people's opinions about you or others or about certain things, that is really quite powerful to be able to change a person's mind. But the only reason those words have so much power is because of the spirit inside those words. What about the mute? All the more support of what I'm saying. As they sign, those are words, but it's not the word itself with the power; it's the spirit, or breath, inside those words that contain the real power. It's the revealing of what's within.

God created everything with His word! One word from God can change everything in our lives, just one word! There is nothing in the Word of God that is without purpose. Every word, every letter, every jot and tittle is not without significance. Even the formation of the letters is important and have meaning.

> For verily I say unto you, Till heaven and
> earth pass, one jot or one tittle shall in no wise
> pass from the law, till all be fulfilled. (Matthew
> 5:18)

The jot is the Greek word ἰῶτα (iōta) which is "the smallest of them all, the Hebrew letter ʼ (yod). Equivalent to the minutest part." The word *tittle* is the Greek word κεραία (keraia) which means "a little horn, extremity, apex, point, the apex of a Hebrew letter." Every part of the Hebrew letters has significance and meaning. In context, Jesus was saying every aspect of the law, even the minutest part, will be fulfilled before heaven and earth pass. But one can also see that every letter and even its formation in its spelling and how it's pronounced is valuable and holds meaning; this is why Jesus pointed to that.

CHAPTER 2

The Sent Word

> He sent his word, and healed them, and delivered *them* from their destructions. (Psalm 107:20)

The reason He sent us His Word is to heal and to deliver. It's not intended for a good story time around the campfire and that's it. No, its intent is to heal and deliver. In order to heal and deliver, there needs to be power.

> For the word of God *is quick*, and *powerful*, and sharper than any twoedged sword, piercing even to the dividing asunder of soul and spirit, and of the joints and marrow, and *is* a discerner of the thoughts and intents of the heart. (Hebrews 4:12)

The word *quick* is not how we think quick as in fast. Quick in the Greek is ζάω (zao); it means "to live, breathe, be among the living. To enjoy real life. To have true life and worthy of the name. Active, blessed, endless in the kingdom of God. Living water, having vital power in itself and exerting the same upon the soul. To be in full vigor. To be fresh, strong, efficient. Active, powerful, efficacious." This word was translated about 143 times, and out of that, it was translated as live 117 times. So the Word of God is full of life, and it is life!

The word *powerful* is the greek word ἐνεργής (Energes) which means "active." This word is from a compound of "en" and "ergon." Where ἐν (en) means "in, by, with." And ἔργον (ergon) means "business, employment, that which any one is occupied. That which one undertakes to do, enterprise, undertaking. Any product whatever, any thing accomplished by hand, art, industry, or mind. An act, deed, thing done."

With these now defined, we can say that the Word of God produces life and is efficient in working life in us. Jesus also said that man shall not *live* (zao) by bread alone but by every word that proceeds from the mouth of God (Matthew 4:4). It is by His word that we live and are healed and are delivered.

We're not talking about a thing; we're talking about a person.

> In the beginning was the Word, and the Word was with God, and the Word was God. (John 1:1)

> But as many as received Him, to them gave He power to become the sons of God, *even* to them that believe on His name: Which were born, not of blood, nor of the will of the flesh, nor of the will of man, but of God. And the Word was made flesh, and dwelt among us, (and we beheld His glory, the glory as of the only begotten of the Father,) full of grace and truth. (John 1:12–14)

All of creation responds to His Word because all of creation was created by His Word. It reaches the very foundation of all creation. We are created, and everything in us was created by His Word. When we hear and receive His Word, our spirit, soul, and body respond. Healing takes effect. All of the molecules within our being take in the word and begin to move around and rearrange for the healing to manifest. The book of Psalms is written in the Old Testament which was written hundreds to a thousand years before Christ. In the 107th chapter and 20th verse of Psalm, it reads in black and white that "He sent His Word and healed them, and delivered them from their destructions." There's more to this than what initially meets the eye. What did the author mean that God sent His Word and healed them?

Now we look at John and combine these scriptures together, and we can see that God was talking about a person, not just a thing like a book. Again, the Word of God, whether it be the Torah or it be the New Testament Scriptures, is all the Word of God and is never just a mere book or some writing. There's so much depth, length, height, and width to the Word. Look at John 1:12 again, "But as many as *received* Him…"

What does it mean to receive? The English definition for received is "be *given*, presented with, or paid something. To come into possession of. To permit to enter. To accept as authoritative, true, or accurate." Just here in the English, without going into the Greek, we can see that in order to receive something, it first must be given. And as it written in Isaiah, "For unto us a child is born, unto us son is *given*: and the government shall be upon his shoulder: and his name shall be called Wonderful, Counsellor, the mighty God, the everlasting Father, the Prince of Peace" (Isaiah 9:6).

A son was given; His Word was sent. Anyone who receives Him He has given him power to become the sons of God. Let's examine the word *sent* from Psalm 107, and the word *given* here in Isaiah 9.

Sent in the English definition means "to cause to go or to be carried from one place or person to another. To dispatch by a means of communication. To cause to issue: such as to pour out."

The etymology of sent comes from Old English *sendan* meaning "send, send forth; throw, impel," causative form of base, *sinþan*, denoting "go, journey" (source of Old English *sið* "way, journey," Old Norse *sinn*, Gothic *sinþs* "going, walk, time") from root *sent*—"to head for, go."

In Hebrew, sent is שָׁלַח (Sahlakh) which means "to send, send away, let go, stretch out. To be sent off, be put away, be divorced, be impelled."

The word *given*, used in Isaiah 9:6, holds the English definition of "presented as a gift, bestowed without compensation."

The etymology of the English word *given* comes from late fourteenth century, "allotted, predestined," past participle adjective from *give*. From 1560s as "admitted, supposed, allowed as a supposition." From late fourteenth century as "disposed, addicted." Middle English also had a noun *give, yeve*, "that which is given or offered freely."

Give is from the Old English *giefan* (West Saxon) "to give, bestow, deliver to another; allot, grant; commit, devote, entrust."

The Hebrew word that was used here is נָתַן (Nathan) which means "to give, bestow, grant, permit, ascribe, employ, devote, consecrate, dedicate, pay wages, sell, exchange, lend, commit, entrust, give over, deliver up, yield produce, occasion, produce, requite to, report, mention, utter, stretch out, extend."

Putting all of this together, a Son, God's Word, Jesus, was given to us. He was sent to us freely without repayment. He was and is the gift presented to us to be received, and as many as would receive Him are given power to become the sons of God. Take notice of the definition of *received* that we covered earlier…in part, it has the meaning of "paid something." What was paid?

> For the wages of sin *is* death; but the gift of God *is* eternal life through Jesus Christ our Lord. (Romans 6:23)

> For he hath made him *to be* sin for us, who knew no sin; that we might be made the righteousness of God in him. (2 Corinthians 5:21)

> For all have sinned, and come short of the glory of God; Being justified freely by his grace through the redemption that is in Christ Jesus. (Romans 3:23–24)

All have sinned, and the wages of our sin is death. But God sent His only begotten, His Son, His Word, that we would be healed and delivered from destruction. The wages of sin was *paid* by Jesus when He became sin for us on the cross and *gave* us freely righteousness in Him! It's for us to receive now. The work of the cross is no longer waiting to be done; it is finished. Take what is so freely given to you. The payment has been settled forever!

The word *wages* in Roman 6:23 is the Greek word ὀψώνιον (opsōnion) which means "a soldier's pay, allowance." Soldiers are on the payroll of the government and are paid by the government's collection of taxes. It was that way then and still is that way today. In Matthew 17, there's a story where Peter was confronted about paying "tribute" or taxes.

> And when they were come to Capernaum, they that received tribute *money* came to Peter, and said, Doth not your master pay tribute? He saith, Yes. And when he was come into the house, Jesus prevented him, saying, What thinkest thou, Simon? of whom do the kings of the earth take custom or tribute? of their own children, or of strangers? Peter saith unto him, Of strangers. Jesus saith unto him, Then are the children free. Notwithstanding, lest we should offend them, go thou to the sea, and cast an hook, and take up the fish that first cometh up; and when thou hast opened his mouth, thou shalt find a piece of money: that take, and give unto them for me and thee. (Matthew 17:24–27)

This encounter shows us that when we rely upon Him and His Word, He supplies all of our need. Due to sin, there was a need; a wage was owed, and this was Jesus showing that He paid the wages of sin. Again, the word *wages* in the Greek is opsōnion, and it means "a soldier's pay." This word comes from ὀψάριον (opsarion) which means "fish," and it was out of the fishes' mouth that Jesus told Peter to draw out the coin to pay the taxes which goes to the state funds which includes the soldiers' wage. As Jonah was the picture of Christ in the belly of the fish, this was a picture of Christ from the belly of a fish paying the wages of sin for man.

The word *delivered* from Psalm 107:20, in the Hebrew, is the word מָלַט (malat) which means "to slip away, escape, deliver, save, be delivered." It could be said this way: "He sent His word and healed them and broke them free causing them to slip from the grip of their destructions." There's another definition that is used with this word, and that is "to give birth to." Jesus said to Nicodemus in John 3:3, "Except a man be born again, he cannot see the kingdom of God." This confounded Nicodemus which caused him to ask "how can this be" which led to one of the more widely familiar pieces of scripture:

> For God so loved the world, that He gave
> His only begotten Son, that whosoever believeth
> in Him should not perish, but have everlasting
> life. (John 3:16)

A kingdom is the domain of a king, hence, king-dom. "Except a man be born again, he cannot see the kingdom of God." Malat is "to give birth to." If we were to change one letter of this word *malat*, מָלַט, the letter ט (tet) which is the last letter reading right to left, to ך (Kaf), we would get this word מֶלֶך (melek) which means "king." The connection of "delivered" and "to give birth to" between the words *king* and *deliver* is off by one letter. It takes a king to deliver and set captives free and to be able to give a new identity thus giving a new birth. It takes a king to give the right and authority to one to be able to have access to all the benefits of the citizenry of that kingdom. It takes a king to give birth to a king.

מָלַט (malat) in the ancient Hebrew looks like this: ⊗ ∠ ᴍ; from the right to left, they are mem, lamed, tet. For the word *king* in the ancient Hebrew, it is ⍟ ∠ ᴍ; again from right to left, they are Mem, Lamed, Kaf. Let's examine the "tet" first. The modern Hebrew symbol ט and the ancient Hebrew ⊗ has the appearance of the bottom of a basket. Some of the meanings of this letter is peace, truth, and good. It is the letter that starts the word *good* in Hebrew which is טוֹב (Tov). It also holds the meaning of "concealed good" as in a pregnancy. The baby inside the mother is hidden within the womb. The soul hidden within the body is another example. "Potential hidden in actual."

The other letter is Kaf which is ך in the modern Hebrew and in the ancient Hebrew is ᴗ which looks like the palm of a hand. One of the meanings of this letter is the power to actualize potential as well as the crown on the head of a prostrated king. The hand is what reveals what we can do. Our hands were made to create, and they have the power to heal. The hands really actualize the potential of a person. It takes the hand of God, the King of kings, to actualize the potential within us. It takes His hand to draw out of us the gifts that He placed within us to reveal that concealed good that is within. The head of a prostrated king is our head. If we can see Jesus in these letters, we should be able to see ourselves in there as well as we are one with Him.

> What is man, that thou art mindful of him?
> and the son of man, that thou visitest him? For
> thou hast made him a little lower than the angels,
> and hast crowned him with glory and honour.
> (Psalm 8:4–5)

> And hath made us kings and priests unto
> God and his Father; to him *be* glory and domin-
> ion for ever and ever. Amen. (Revelation 1:6)

It is our crowned head that prostrates before our great King, and in doing, He so He exalts us in due season with more honor, glory, favor, healing etc… Healing is something that is already inside of us. If you were to somehow receive a cut, see what happens over a couple of days. The cut will be on the mend immediately after the injury happened. It takes the hand of God to draw out that healing from a person. Anybody who says Jesus is Lord is the body of Christ and therefore is His feet and His hands, and He can, will, and does work through His body even through the laying on of hands.

The prostrated crowned head is also a picture of Jesus who yielded to the plan of the Father and laid down His own life. The English definition of prostrate is "lay oneself flat on the ground face downward, especially in reverence or submission." A second definition is "of distress, exhaustion, or illness, reduce someone to extreme physical weakness." In the garden of Gethsemane, Jesus is seen in agony, but regardless of the pain, He still went with the plan of God.

> And he was withdrawn from them about a stone's cast, and kneeled down, and prayed, Saying, Father, if thou be willing, remove this cup from me: nevertheless not my will, but thine, be done. And there appeared an angel unto him from heaven, strengthening him. And being in an agony he prayed more earnestly: and his sweat was as it were great drops of blood falling down to the ground. (Luke 22:41–44)

We examined the last letters of these two words; let's look at the two first letters that unite them: מל. The letter on the right is the Mem, and the one on the left is the Lamed. When these two letters are put together, you get the definition: "Word, continuation, a chain of words blended together to form sentences, a continuation of segments, which fill the whole." Ecclesiastes 8:4 says, "Where the word of the king is there is power…"

> He sent his word, and healed them, and delivered *them* from their destructions. (Psalm 107:20)

CHAPTER 3

In the Beginning: Aleph

> In the beginning was the Word, and the Word was with God, and the Word was God. (John 1:1)

What a profound revelation from John! Stop and think on this for a moment, and let it really sink in who we are talking about here. Get a picture of the Word being with God in the very beginning before the earth ever was. What comes to my mind is Proverbs 8.

> I was set up from everlasting, from the beginning, or ever the earth was. When *there were* no depths, I was brought forth; when *there were* no fountains abounding with water. Before the mountains were settled, before the hills was I brought forth: While as yet he had not made the earth, nor the fields, nor the highest part of the dust of the world. When he prepared the heavens, I was there: when he set a compass upon the face of the depth: When he established the clouds above: when he strengthened the fountains of the deep: When he gave to the sea his decree, that the waters should not pass his commandment: when he appointed the foundations of the earth: Then

> I was by him, *as* one brought up *with him*: and I
> was daily *his* delight, rejoicing always before him.
> (<u>Proverbs 8:23–30)</u>

This Proverb is "wisdom" talking, which is truly Jesus talking. Paul said in 1 Corinthians 1:24: "Christ the power of God, and the *wisdom* of God." And here, He says that He was daily His delight, rejoicing always before Him. Then my mind goes to Calvary. It's truly a sobering thought that He who knew no sin became sin for us (2 Corinthians 5:21). He was daily His delight, and yet, as we studied previously, He was sent, or in other words, divorced from God for our sakes.

> But made himself of no reputation, and
> took upon him the form of a servant, and was
> made in the likeness of men: And being found
> in fashion as a man, he humbled himself, and
> became obedient unto death, even the death of
> the cross. (Philippians 2:7–8)

First Corinthians 1:23 says, "But we preach Christ crucified…"—the wisdom and power of God crucified (Selah).

> I am Alpha and Omega, the beginning
> and the ending, saith the Lord, which is, and
> which was, and which is to come, the Almighty.
> (<u>Revelation 1:8)</u>

This is Jesus talking in this verse. He was talking to John while he was on the island of Patmos. In this Greek translation, it reads Alpha and Omega, which is to say I am the first and the last. After reading Proverbs 8 and identifying that as being Jesus, it would make sense that He would be the first and the last. He was there before anything ever was, and according to Isaiah 9, He is also the "Everlasting."

However, John is not a Greek speaker; he would have been a Hebrew speaker, and I have no reason to believe that Jesus would have spoken to him in any other language than Hebrew, so I believe Jesus would have said to John, "I am the Aleph and the Tov." The meaning is still the same here with the first and the last. Alpha is to Aleph as it is to *A* in the English alphabet. Omega is to Tov as it is to *Z* in the English alphabet. I am the first and the last.

However, Greek is far more expressive in its words than English, and the Hebrew goes even beyond that. I believe that the Jewish language was specifically given to the Jewish people specifically by God, and within their language is the secret of creation. It's the language that God used to create everything we see and everything we don't see. It's a language that is made up of words just like everyone else, but their language is structured more like a person more than any other language. The complexity of Hebrew is likened more to a person than just plain speech. For example, we are made up of three major parts: spirit, soul, and body. The Hebrew language is built the same. One letter has form, name, and number—three parts, just like a person. One letter has its very own meaning made up of other parts of the Hebrew alphabet. Quite a masterful design by quite the Masterful Designer. So a word in Hebrew is dripping in revelation hidden within its formations inside each and every letter within one word. Therefore, when Jesus says that He is the Aleph and the Tov, He is actually saying so much more than "I am the first and the last" however true that may be.

It's no coincidence that the book of Revelation is called the book of Revelation. It is not, however, a revelation of only the end-time and what is to take place in the future. It's really the book of Revelation of *Jesus Christ*. It's really about Him. I believe it's the revelation of Jesus Christ that will get believers through the end-times not only for those who are here after the rapture but also even now as we go through the end of times.

Here is one of the revelations of Jesus Christ, and it's a big one! That He is the Aleph and the Tov. He is the very word that proceeds from the mouth of God.

But he answered and said, It is written,
Man shall not live by bread alone, but by every

word that proceedeth out of the mouth of God.
(Matthew 4:4)

Abide in me, and I in you. As the branch
cannot bear fruit of itself, except it abide in the
vine; no more can ye, except ye abide in me. I am
the vine, ye *are* the branches: He that abideth in
me, and I in him, the same bringeth forth much
fruit: for *without me ye can do nothing.* (John
15:4–5)

For the LORD giveth wisdom: out of his
mouth *cometh* knowledge and understanding.
(Proverbs 2:6)

We live by every word that comes from the mouth of God. He
sent and gave His Word, His Son; He is the Word of God whose
glory we beheld as the only begotten of the Father who manifested
in the flesh, and without Him, we can do nothing. The Father gave
the Hebrew language to the Jewish people, and within that language
was the Messiah concealed from all flesh until the appointed time for
Him to be revealed. Here, He is saying that "He is every word that
proceeded form the mouth of God and all of those Hebrew letters—
the aleph, the tov, and everything in between—point to Him. By
those Words, by Him, all things were created."

Who is the image of the invisible God, the
firstborn of every creature: For by him were all
things created, that are in heaven, and that are
in earth, visible and invisible, whether *they be*
thrones, or dominions, or principalities, or powers: all things were created by him, and for him.
(Colossians 1:15–16)

The aleph is the first letter in the Hebrew alphabet, and it looks
like this א.

The Tov is the last letter in the Hebrew alphabet, and it looks like this ת.

John 1:1 says, "In the beginning was the Word…" Familiar start…

> In the beginning God created the heaven and the earth. (<u>Genesis 1:1</u>)

Here's what that verse looks like in the Hebrew:

הָאָרֶץ וְאֵת הַשָּׁמַיִם אֵת אֱלֹהִים בָּרָא בְּרֵאשִׁית
h'eretz v'et h'shamim et Elohim Bara Beresheet

When reading Hebrew, it is read from the right to the left. I provided the transliteration of the Hebrew under the Hebrew words so you could see what those words are.

The first word is Beresheet which means "beginning." The actual word is without the Bet, or the B, in front. The *B* was added.

The second word is Bara which means "create."

Elohim is next which means "rulers, judges, God."

Now look at this word here: הַשָּׁמַיִם This means "the heavens," *H'shamim*. Heavens is Shamim (שָׁמַיִם), so when the Hei (ה) is added to the front, it is "the," therefore, "the heavens." The same thing is applied to "the earth"—הָאָרֶץ (h'eretz). Take away the Hei (ה), and you have Eretz (אֶרֶץ) which means earth. Place the Hei in front, then you have "the earth."

Now look at the word *et* (אֵת). Do these letters look familiar to you? It's the Aleph Tov! There is no translation for this word in the English, and it is not "the" as that's what the Hei is for. So it doesn't actually make sense why it's there…except that it's Jesus—the Word of God in the beginning with God the Aleph and the Tov!

If this isn't enough to demonstrate that Jesus is the Aleph Tov, the Word of God, let's examine the aleph and the tov just a little further.

Aleph א 𐤀. This letter represents strength and power, and its ancient Hebrew symbol is an ox head. An ox is full of power and strength. The ox was used to work the field. A yoke would be placed around its neck, and it would either plow the field or it would tread out the grain. The yoke would fit on another smaller, and younger, ox attached to the bigger and older ox. The yoke would keep the smaller attached to the bigger, so even if the smaller ox got distracted in the work, it couldn't go anywhere because it was attached to the much stronger ox who would keep the work going. This yoke would train the smaller ox to do the work when it got older and stronger, and that same ox would eventually be doing the same for the new generation of working ox.

If you look close at the modern aleph א)), there's a stem on the right and the left with a connection in the middle. Each of these pieces are actually other Hebrew letters. The "stems" are yods. A yod looks like this: י. It is a very tiny letter. It's the smallest of letters in the Hebrew alphabet. You cannot make any of the Hebrew letters without the yod. Neither can you end any of the letters without the yod—the font for Hebrew within this book; you don't really see the yod in the Hebrew letters too clearly, but if you look at the Torah or even a concordance, look closely at the Hebrew letters, and you will see a slight flip up on the top of the letter. That is the yod. When you write with a pen, there's a little mark that goes before the letter you want to write, and when you lift the pen, there's a little mark again as the pen is lifted from the page; this is the yod. So aleph has the yod on the right, and there's a yod on the left, but it's inverted, and the center? That is a vav which looks like this: ו. The vav literally means "connection," and that's what the letter does in the Hebrew language; it is used as an "and." Here, the vav is connecting the two yods in the modern Hebrew letter aleph.

Look again at the ancient Hebrew letter for aleph 𐤀. It looks like an ox head. It almost has the same structure as the modern aleph, but only there's no vav in the center. Rather, it's more of the Samech in Hebrew, and that letter looks like this: ס. The samech is connecting the two yods together. Why the change? There was a massive shift that took place in Genesis which changed all of creation. It impacted everything we see and don't see.

When we study the Word and are finding Jesus in the letters and the words, we will discover us in there as well. Remember what is said in Acts 17:28: "For *in Him* we live, and move, and have our being…" When we begin to see Jesus as Messiah, we begin to really see ourselves.

ע See the two yods placed at the top of the samech. The yod is an arm ‌‌ in the ancient Hebrew, and it literally means "arm and hand" in its definition.

> Who has believed our report? And to whom has *the arm of the Lord* been revealed? For he shall grow up before him as a tender plant, and as a root out of a dry ground: he hath no form nor comeliness; and when we shall see him, *there* is no beauty that we should desire him. He is despised and rejected of men; a man of sorrows, and acquainted with grief: and we hid as it were *our* faces from him; he was despised, and we esteemed him not. Surely he hath borne our griefs, and carried our sorrows: yet we did esteem him stricken, smitten of God, and afflicted. But he *was* wounded for our transgressions, *he was* bruised for our iniquities: the chastisement of our peace *was* upon him; and with his stripes we are healed. (Isaiah 53:1–5)

This is the Messiah passage. It points beautifully to Jesus! "No form nor comeliness; and when we shall see Him, there is no beauty that we should desire Him." He looks just like a regular guy in His day. Not someone with outstanding features that makes Him stand out in the crowd. His spirit sure made Him stand out in the crowd, but just the natural appearance of Him was quite regular. People were astonished when they found out that it was true that He is Mashiach. They were expecting someone else. A military hero or someone that would "fit the part" a little better. But no…They got a boy that was born in a manger that looked like the rest of them. Jesus was born

Jew, so He would have looked Jewish. He was not from Africa nor from Sweden. He was a Jewish boy who followed all the precepts as everyone else did in His region until He fulfilled them all, that is.

"We hid our face from him…" During the time of His capture, His disciples were scattered, and He was alone. Some even rejected Him when people confronted them about their associations with Christ.

"We did esteem Him stricken, smitten of God, and afflicted." There on the cross, He was beaten to literal shreds looking smitten of God and afflicted.

Verse 5 says, "With His stripes we are healed." He sent His Word and healed them and delivered them from their destructions. It just happened in a way nobody was expecting. This whole segment speaks of Jesus!

Now we're talking about the yod in connection to the aleph. Look how it all starts in the first verse: "To whom has the arm of the Lord been revealed?" Then it goes right into, "For he shall grow up before him as a tender plant…" He? Who is He? The arm of the Lord. Not everyone believed upon Jesus as Messiah; even so it is today…to whom has the arm of the Lord been revealed? Who has seen the arm of the Lord, but those whose eyes and ears have been opened? Whom once were blind but now can see. Whom once were deaf and now can hear. Jesus is the arm of the Lord, and it takes a revealing by His Spirit for us to see Him. It is by His Spirit that His arm, Jesus, is revealed. The yod in the ancient Hebrew is ﻭ, and it is the picture of an arm and a hand.

> And God said, Let us make man in our image, after our likeness: and let them have dominion over the fish of the sea, and over the fowl of the air, and over the cattle, and over all the earth, and over every creeping thing that creepeth upon the earth. So God created man in his *own* image, in the image of God created he him; male and female created he them. (Genesis 1:26–27)

In the Hebrew, the word *likeness*, demut, means "similitude (which means the quality or the state of being similar to something), in the likeness of, like as." This word comes from dama which means "to be like, resemble." Man was made to resemble God. We look just like Him. Of course, we are a little lower than Him because we are the created, and He is the Creator. We have His DNA, but without Him, we are nothing. So look at the ancient Hebrew aleph: 𐤀.

Notice how one yod is slightly lower than the other yod. Jesus is the arm of the Lord, and by Him, all things exist. We just look like Him but a little lower. These yods, again, are connected by the samech: ס. This letter is like a circle, and its meaning is "to support." Its formation is a circle and also holds the meaning of a "wedding ring." What are wedding rings used for? To mark a covenant that has been made between a man a woman—a covenant that they will support one another and they have been made one flesh. It's a symbol of eternity because once the bond is made, it is made forever just like the circle; it just continues with no end. So these yods are married, one to the other. They are bonded together by a covenant that was made by God before the earth ever was.

> But with the precious blood of Christ, as of a lamb without blemish and without spot: Who verily was *foreordained before the foundation of the world*, but was manifest in these last times for you. (1 Peter 1:19–20)

> And all that dwell upon the earth shall worship him, whose names are not written in the book of life of *the Lamb slain from the foundation of the world*. (Revelation 13:8)

From before the very beginning, God made a covenant with man. He made a promise to be connected with man forever. He made up His mind what He wanted, and He went forward with it. He left the decision up to us after that. He allowed us to make the decision whether we want the same relationship with Him or not. The choice was ours and even still is ours. He connected us to Him by a promise, then He created us. This Yod was made a little lower than the main Yod connected by the Samech—wedding ring of promise, a covenant.

Then a change happened. Sin entered in by the following of another voice. Satan led man to eat the fruit which we were not to eat from. In doing so, we disconnected ourselves from the relationship God had set up for us to have with Him. There was so much more to learn and develop with Him, but the enemy got to us early. So our thoughts toward God had changed. The way we think and see Him and ourselves changed. We felt we had to hide ourselves from Him and run from His presence even just at the sound of Him walking through the garden. The Lord came along and spoke of the covenant that He had made and that He will deliver on His promise:

> And I will put enmity between thee and the
> woman, and between thy seed and her seed; it
> shall bruise thy head, and thou shalt bruise his
> heel. (Genesis 3:15)

He brought up the wedding vows even though we did not keep any. He stated the covenant that was made and will become manifest in due season, and then He mentions what the repercussions would be from the decisions we made. Yet He so gracefully assured us that He would cover us and would make all things right:

> Unto Adam also and to his wife did the
> LORD God make coats of skins, and clothed
> them. (Genesis 3:21)

Us trying to clothe ourselves with fig leaves was entirely inadequate. He clothed us Himself in saying that He will clothe us in righteousness and remember our sin no more.

The relationship had changed. We could no longer approach Him the way that we could have in the garden. There was sin to deal with now and a sin consciousness. We need a mediator at this point in order for our relationship to get back intact, and that's exactly what God set up for us from the foundation of the world.

Now we go from the samech connecting the yods—the wedding band connecting the yods to needing a connector to get us back to God.

Let's compare the modern aleph with the Ancient for a moment.

אַ

The modern on the left and the ancient on the right. The ancient had the two yods somewhat in the same direction, just one a little lower than the other. The modern still has the yods, just one is inverted now and connected by the vav versus the samech.

The inverted yod speaks to the change that happened in the garden. Now please don't misunderstand what I am saying using the Hebrew letters. There is no bad letter as God did not create bad; He only created good. The Hebrew language is God's language, and therefore, everything about the language is good. With respect to the story of the fall of man, I am in no way implying that the Hebrew language is cursed but, quite the contrary, that it tells the whole story of creation and more! There are secrets even now hidden within the language. But God is beginning to open more, revealing Jesus and some of the "secrets" of creation.

The inverted yod speaks to the fall of man. We were a little lower than Elohim, and now have been inverted. We look like Him, but there's been a change.

> What is man, that thou art mindful of him?
> and the son of man, that thou visitest him? For
> thou hast made him a little lower than the angels,
> and hast crowned him with glory and honour.
> (Psalm 8:4–5)

The word *angels* in this verse is the word *Elohim* which can mean angels or gods but is mostly used as a name for God.

In the garden, the relationship was established by absolute grace. God chose man! The connection was a covenant connection established by God Himself. When the fall happened, the samech was broken, and we could only get to God through works. That's where the vav comes in.

The vav is the sixth letter in the Hebrew alphabet. This number is known as man's number, and it is the number associated with work as seen in Genesis when God completed all His work in six days. Now, there's way more to vav than this, but we will stay on our purpose for examining vav for this discourse.

It would now take some work for us to get to God. We need to do some things in order to see Him. Over time, the law came to the Jews and laid out exact things to do in order to keep the heart and mind pure for the relationship with God to remain intact. Come to find out we were trying to cover ourselves again in fig leaves so He sent us His Son as He promised He would. He came as that connection for us to get to God! He is that Vav! In the ancient Hebrew, the vav looks like this: Y. It looks somewhat like a tent peg. The purpose of a tent peg is to keep the ropes attached to the tents. In other words, it was to keep the covering over the occupants within the tent. See, Jesus is the one who holds all things together. He holds our relationship with God intact and will not let it slip. His finished works is more than enough. This Vav keeps the two yods together even if one yod is inverted. This reminds me of what the psalmist said in Psalm 139:8: "If I ascend up into heaven, thou *art* there: if I make my bed in hell, behold, thou *art there*." No matter the circumstance or the situation, He will never leave you or forsake you, for the finished works of Jesus are enough to satisfy any work that's needed to approach God!

Now that Jesus had finished the work, taking the place of the Vav, and connecting us to God, again, we are now back to a grace relationship with the Lord! Ephesians 2:8 says, "For by grace are ye saved through faith; and that not of yourselves: *it is* the gift of God." So the samech relationship is restored; only now, we have a better covenant established upon better promises according to Hebrews 8:6: "But now hath he obtained a more excellent ministry, by how much also *he is the mediator of a better covenant, which was established upon better promises.*"

Let's look again at the samech: ס. In the ancient Hebrew, it looks like this: ꓤ. The name for this letter is "Thorn."

> And they clothed him with purple, and platted a crown of thorns, and put it about his *head.* (<u>Mark 15:17</u>)

They placed a crown of thorns upon Jesus's head… The samech in ancient Hebrew is a thorn. This speaks to His eternal place as our mediator with God that no one and nothing can remove!

> Who shall separate us from the love of Christ? *shall* tribulation, or distress, or persecution, or famine, or nakedness, or peril, or sword? As it is written, For thy sake we are killed all the day long; we are accounted as sheep for the slaughter. Nay, in all these things we are more than conquerors through him that loved us. For I am persuaded, that neither death, nor life, nor angels, nor principalities, nor powers, nor things present, nor things to come, Nor height, nor depth, nor any other creature, shall be able to separate us from the love of God, which is in Christ Jesus our Lord. (<u>Romans 8:35–39</u>)

This covenant is not a covenant that we uphold. It's a covenant that is between the Father and the Son. We are the fruit of that covenant between them. Christ is seated forever at the right hand of God, and those who are *in* Christ are seated with Him forever. If it was a covenant between God and man, we would still need sacrifice, but thank God that it is not! It is settled once and for all!

CHAPTER 4

In the Beginning: Tov

Tov (ת) **✝**. As you can see, the ancient Hebrew pictograph for tov is two crossed sticks. It means "mark, token, sign, signal. It is also known to be called a "stamp" or "the seal of creation." In Aramaic, the word *tov* means "more," and in Hebrew, it means "good."

This letter, just like the aleph that we examined, is made up of other letters of the Hebrew alphabet. As we've already discussed, all letters, with the exception of the yod, are made up of other Hebrew letters. The tov has two other letters in it: daleth and nun.

The dalet looks like this ד and the ancient Hebrew **▽**.

The nun looks like this נ and the ancient Hebrew **⌐**.

The ancient Hebrew pictograph for dalet is a door, and it means "entrance, door, move, lifting up, elevation." The definition "move" is there because the door "moves" upon its hinges to open and close. The Talmud is defined as the basic collection of detailed and concise writings of Jewish law and thought. It is full of questions and answers between rabbis discussing different scenarios and how the Law would apply to those scenarios. In the Talmud, it says that the dalet also means poor. The gimel, which is the letter that comes before the dalet, is the rich man giving to the poor man—the dalet. The formation of the dalet is said to have the foot toward the gimel to receive alms, thus the "move" aspect of dalet as well. The "poor man" must always be ready to move to receive from the "rich man."

> *I am the door*: by me if any man enter in, he shall be saved, and shall go in and out, and find pasture. (John 10:9)

> For ye know the grace of our Lord Jesus Christ, that, though he was rich, yet *for your sakes he became poor*, that ye through his poverty might be rich. (1 Corinthians 8:9)

> But made himself of no reputation, and took upon him the form of a servant, and was made in the likeness of men: And being found in fashion as a man, he humbled himself, and became obedient unto death, even the death of the cross. Wherefore God also hath highly exalted him, and given him a name which is above every name. (Philippians 2:7–9)

Jesus is the door, and He became poor; Jesus is the Dalet! The verse here in Philippians demonstrates the Talmud's insights of the Dalet. The word *reputation* here is κενόω (kenoo) which means "to empty, to make empty." Coming from all glory and putting on the likeness of men would be "becoming poor." This is great humility to do something like that surely! So now we can see Jesus leaving behind what He only knew to become like us. Poor and rich is relative and is in the eye of the beholder. It is not defined by some number or value. If there are comparisons, it would be easier to identify what is rich and what is poor.

If we could possibly imagine what it is like to be in the full presence of God and knowing nothing else but that, then becoming just a mere man (in which I am not saying that Jesus was not divine) that would, in comparison, be poor. Now that He is poor—so that we would be rich, throughout His post womb, pre-cross ministry—He relied fully on God. How many times did He go to God in prayer? He showed us to do the same. On the cross, Jesus bore the sin of us all. That's quite poor. More than that, God turned from Him on that cross. It was the poor Dalet reaching out to the rich, God the Gimmel, as it was recorded in Matthew 27:46: "Eli, Eli, lama sabachthani? that is to say, My God, my God, why hast thou forsaken me?" This word *forsaken* in the Greek is ἐγκαταλείπω (eng-kat-al-i'-po) which means "abandon, desert, leave helpless, totally abandoned, utterly forsaken, to leave behind." The root of this word is a compound from kata and leipo λείπω (leipo) which means "to be destitute, to be wanting." God left him destitute and poor so that He would never turn His back on us. Jesus was that Dalet reaching out to the Gimmel in saying, "My God, My God, why hast thou forsaken Me?"

Notice in the meaning of the word *dalet* that we mentioned above, "Lifting up, elevation." Jesus humbled Himself, and God exalted Him! The word there, "exalt", is ὑπερυψόω (hooperoopsoo) which means "to exalt to the highest rank and power. To be *lifted up* with pride, exalted beyond measure." The word *exalt* in English means "to raise in rank, power or character. To raise high, to *elevate.*" The Gimmel giving to the Dalet! The Dalet reached out to the Gimmel with the hand of obedience, and the Gimmel gave and lifted up the Dalet. The form of dalet also holds the meaning of "willingness to sacrifice one's life for one's people" and "the door as the entrance way to the truth."

The Hebrew letter nun in the ancient Hebrew is a picture of a seed sprout. It holds the meanings of continuation, fish, kingdom, heir to the throne. The modern form of this letter represents a "bent-over servant." The bent-over servant is the yielded servant. Now Jesus is indeed the beloved Son, but while He was conducting the "cross ministry," he was a yielded servant. Remember what Jesus said in the garden of Gethsemane.

> Saying, Father, if thou be willing, remove this cup from me: nevertheless not my will, but thine, be done.(Luke 22:42)

Jesus came and began the work of establishing a new kingdom. This is in part why the leadership of the time were so afraid of His arrival. They thought a great and mighty warrior king had come to remove them from office. So they did everything they could to eliminate Him without knowing who He was. When they heard it was Jesus of Nazareth, the son of Joseph, they all mocked. They didn't believe it! They would even say, "Can anything good come from Nazareth?" Well, once the miracles started happening and the crowds started drawing near to Him, that was when He started to get the attention of the religious leaders of the time. Now they were on a mission to destroy Him! The ruling party of Israel really didn't take an interest in getting Jesus because, to them, He really wasn't a threat, so why waste the time and resources to going after some street preacher? Little did any of them know who they were truly dealing with.

> Which none of the princes of this world knew: for had they known *it*, they would not have crucified the Lord of glory. (1 Corinthians 2:8)

There are a variety of scriptures that record Jesus talking about the establishing of a new kingdom. He wasn't talking about the overthrowing of Rome or Caesar. He was talking about a heavenly, spiritual kingdom that would endure forever. Jesus took very little concern where the Roman occupancy was concerned. He even told the people to pay to Caesar what is Caesar's.

> And Jesus answering said unto them, Render to Caesar the things that are Caesar's, and to God the things that are God's. And they marvelled at him. (Mark 12:17)

The first part of what He said in this verse showed the very little concern He took up with Roman occupancy. He could have talked about how the people need to stand up against Caesar and fight for their rights! Take up arms and beat their shields! He could have rallied the troops to fight tyranny and injustice from the Roman government. He could have rallied the troops to fight for freedom. Instead, render to Caesar what is his…In other words, "eh" (*Enter shoulder shrug here*). But look at the latter of this verse: "…and to God the things that are God's." Jesus was not here to overthrow the Roman Empire but the empire of the evil one. He was here to establish a new kingdom of soft hearts toward God—a kingdom that would endure for eternity.

Again, one of the meanings of this letter is fish. Fish is a symbol of reproductivity.

> But as many as received him, to them gave
> he power to become the *sons* of God, *even* to
> them that believe on his name. (John 1:12)

The word *son* in Hebrew is בֵּן (Ben). This is comprised of two letters bet and nun. The bet is a picture of a tent in the ancient Hebrew: ⍁ and this means house. So when you place these two letters together, you get "the continuation of the house." A son continues the lineage. Therefore, when we receive Christ, we have the power to become sons, rather, a continuation of the house and kingdom of God.

There, we have these two letters within the tov with so much meaning and depth to them; the study of these letters would take an eternity to learn as I believe it is because we are learning about a person not just simply a communication tool.

The dalet is the door, and the nun is the kingdom. And these together make up the modern form of the tov. Jesus is the door to the kingdom. And the word *tov* literally means "good." When the poor, dalet, is informed that they can enter into a kingdom, nun, where all their needs would be met and would have life abundantly and would continue therein for eternity, I would say that is *good* news! Good news is the definition for Gospel!

> The Spirit of the Lord is upon me, because
> he hath anointed me to preach the *gospel to the
> poor*; he hath sent me to heal the brokenhearted,

to preach deliverance to the captives, and recovering of sight to the blind, to set at liberty them
that are bruised. (Luke 4:18)

I just point out the "gospel to the poor" because it is there in plain English, but reading the whole thing is good news! The brokenhearted healed, that is good news! Captives delivered, that is good news! The blind can see; that is good news! The bruised are liberated; that is Good news!

The crossed sticks of the ancient Hebrew tov and the ox head of the aleph:

$$+ \, \aleph$$

Again, the aleph, ox head, means strength, and the tov, crossed sticks, means sign. I don't think it's coincidental that the tov is the cross. Even if one would say Jesus was really crucified on a pole, not a cross, you know what the cross stands for anyway.

> *But we preach Christ crucified*, unto the Jews
> a stumbling block, and unto the Greeks foolishness; But unto them which are called, both Jews
> and Greeks, *Christ the power of God, and the wisdom of God*. (1 Corinthians 1:23–24)

Power is also strength, so here it is in ancient Hebrew: Christ is the strength and power of God crucified as a mark, a sign, a symbol that all your sins have been dealt with on the cross. We are reunited with the Father as though sin had never happened! We now have this access to the Father whereby we can approach Him without concern of Him accepting us or not! We are accepted in the Beloved for eternity!

CHAPTER 5

Expectation

And the people spake against God, and against Moses, Wherefore have ye brought us up out of Egypt to die in the wilderness? for *there is* no bread, neither *is there any* water; and our soul loatheth this light bread. And the LORD sent fiery serpents among the people, and they bit the people; and much people of Israel died. Therefore the people came to Moses, and said, We have sinned, for we have spoken against the LORD, and against thee; pray unto the LORD, that he take away the serpents from us. And Moses prayed for the people. And the LORD said unto Moses, Make thee a fiery serpent, and set it upon a pole: and it shall come to pass, that every one that is bitten, when he looketh upon it, shall live. And Moses made a serpent of brass, and put it upon a pole, and it came to pass, that if a serpent had bitten any man, when he beheld the serpent of brass, he lived. (<u>Numbers 21:5–9</u>)

When the people said to Moses, "We have sinned," the word sinned is חָטָא (khaw-taw), and it means "to miss the mark, go wrong, forfeit." They complained about God and His provision in saying, "We loathe this light bread," and "Did you bring us here to die?" Well, for some, they did die in the wilderness, but that certainly was not why God brought them there. You can see how God led them out of Egypt by a cloud during the day and fire by night and fed them by His own hand with manna and with quail, yet they complained about His provisions and guidance. But this is not just a Jewish problem. This is a human problem. It's easy to blame the Israelites for unbelief when we see what God did for them on the finished end of the work.

It's really no different today when people blame God for their trouble even when He is providing through circumstances and turns the circumstances around. These people repent and go the right way then when things are going well, just not as well as they thought; they blame God for it not being better than what it was when there was a life in captivity. You know a life of the world and sin is a life of captivity, no different than when the Jewish people were slaves in Egypt and subject to hard labor. Proverbs 13:15 says, "The way of the transgressor is hard."

The Israelites eventually admitted that they were wrong in how they spoke against God and Moses. That's the first step to getting right: recognize one's wrong. An addict can't get help unless it is realized that there is a problem and help is needed. The works of the flesh is an addiction, and it's an addiction that should be and can be broken from one's life. We must first recognize that there is a problem and that we need help to get rid of the problem and then turn to the right help to get free, which is Jesus!

The people of Israel recognized the problem, and they admitted it to Moses and asked for help. God told Moses what to do, and I find these things he did to be so fascinating. God told Moses, as you've already read, to make a fiery serpent of brass and set it on a pole. Let's examine some of these words.

Fiery is שָׂרָף (saw-rawf) which means "poisonous serpent." The "fiery" name is due to the burning effects of the poison and the root word of sawrawf is שָׂרַף (saw-raf) which means "to burn."

Serpent is נָחָשׁ (naw-khawsh) which means "serpent, snake." The root of the word is נָחַשׁ (naw-khash) which means "to practice divination, observe signs, learn by experience, to observe signs or omens." I find these words intriguing, and it causes me to consider why did it have to be serpents as the result of their speech?

In Genesis 3:1, we have the first mention of the word *serpent,* and it is the same word for serpent that is used here in Numbers.

> Now the serpent was more subtil than any
> beast of the field which the LORD God had made.
> And he said unto the woman, Yea, hath God
> said, Ye shall not eat of every tree of the garden?
> (Genesis 3:1)

The word *subtil* means "shrewd and crafty." The serpent was intelligent and observant. The serpent came and questioned what it was that God had told Adam and Eve. However, we must remember that this book—the Bible, the whole Bible, Old and New Testament—is more than a natural book. The Word of God is indeed a spiritual book. Therefore, we should be reminded that the things that took place in the Word as being illustrated naturally all took place spiritually and is either the result of something that already took place in the spirit or an illustration of what will take place in the spirit.

Seeing this serpent speaking to Eve, I do not think that it was simply a talking snake beguiling the woman, but it was the voice of Lucifer who was inside the serpent. The serpent yielded itself to Lucifer and became a voice and a body for him to operate in the earth in order to speak to man. It was not the snake trying to deceive man but the spirit that was inside the snake to deceive man. This is why when the punishments were given to the serpent, he was told in verse 14, "Because thou hast done this, thou *art* cursed above all cattle, and above every beast of the field; upon thy belly shalt thou go, and dust shalt thou eat all the days of thy life." There was a curse immediately placed upon the serpent for yielding to Lucifer. Then in verse 15 it says, "And I will put enmity between thee and the woman, and between thy seed and her seed; it shall bruise thy head, and thou shalt bruise his heel." God was not telling the snake itself that there is going to be enmity between the man and the snake, but God was speaking in the spirit to the spirit, Lucifer, inside the serpent.

In verses 4 and 5, the serpent questions God's providence for man.

> And the serpent said unto the woman, Ye shall not surely die: For God doth know that in the day ye eat thereof, then your eyes shall be opened, and ye shall be as gods, knowing good and evil. (Genesis 3:4–5)

> And when the woman saw that the tree *was* good for food, and that it *was* pleasant to the eyes, and a tree to be desired to make *one* wise, she took of the fruit thereof, and did eat, and gave also unto her husband with her; and he did eat. (Genesis 3:6)

Notice how she saw that tree was good for food, pleasant to the eyes, and to be desired to make one wise. As if there wasn't enough food in the garden that was pleasant to the eyes and as if they weren't endowed with enough wisdom, although man was given the place to name all the animals. That would take some wisdom to take on a tremendous task as such! The point here is the questioning of Gods providence for His people. Regardless of all of the provision and the open diet plan with exception to one tree, it wasn't good enough. The ploy was effective in its working in saying, "God is leaving something good out from you because He doesn't want you to have something." "Did He really say not to eat of the tree?" "Well, He is only saying that because He does not want you to be like Him." Out of fear of missing out, they complied, much like the serpent complied. Look again at the root word for serpent in the Hebrew: נָחַשׁ (nawkhash) which, in part, means "to practice divination." What is divination? "The art or practice that seeks to foresee or foretell future events or discover hidden knowledge usually by the interpretation of omens or by the aid of supernatural powers." The "desire to make one wise" is a form of divination. Behind the word *serpent* is the word *divination*. Behind this serpent was the diviner.

The serpents in Numbers came along as a sign that the Jewish people were yielding to the same sin as Adam and Eve: the questioning of God's providence for His people. They murmured about how God was dealing with them—ignoring all of the good He did and only looking at one aspect of the situation. The serpents were a representation of what was really already happening in the spirit. They were already bitten by a serpent, and the hearts were slowly dying as they were turning from God. Then it happened in the natural realm… The questioning of God's providence is like a poison that slowly infects the person until they follow other gods or no longer believe that there is even a God.

Before we go into verse 8, let's examine verse 9 of Numbers 21. "Moses made a serpent of *brass* and put it upon a pole…" The word *brass* here in Hebrew is נְחֹשֶׁת (nekh-o'-sheth) which means "copper, brass, lust, harlotry." There was a lust for other things, and the obeying the other voice was harlotry. In the *Strong's*, for this Hebrew word, the meaning "lust and harlotry" were identified as being dubious, which means where it comes from is unknown and doubtful. Although the definition, lust and harlotry, as some of the meanings of this word, are dubious, what caught my attention was the people of Israel at that time were actually acting dubious. Dubious means "unsettled in opinion, doubtful." They were unsettled in their opinion of God and His providence, and that leads to dangerous things down the road. This serpent that Moses made was made of brass—a symbol of the doubt. Furthermore, brass in the English definition means "an alloy consisting essentially of copper and zinc in variable proportions." An alloy is a mixture of two or more metals or of a metal and a nonmetal. One of the definitions that is provided as well is "an admixture that lessens value."

> I know thy works, that thou art neither
> cold nor hot: I would thou wert cold or hot. So
> then because thou art lukewarm, and neither

cold nor hot, I will spue thee out of my mouth.
(Revelation 3:15–16)

There is either cold or hot unless you mix the two then you get lukewarm. Many people get lukewarm due to mixture taking place in one's heart concerning the things of God. This is what happened in the garden. Adam and Eve had initially one thought toward God, and that would be, I presume, He is a God of abundance and supply. Simply by looking at what God had given them and prepared for them even before they were created. There was nothing there to indicate to them that God would be bad to them or that there was even bad in the earth aside from the tree of knowledge of good and evil. This was the one thing where "bad" was concerned as the eating of the fruit of the tree came with a grave consequence. Outside of that one tree, there was nothing else that pointed to bad! Until this voice of a stranger showed up, and we obeyed that voice. Once that happened, it was a double mind that was created, and a mixture of thoughts flooded our minds about the Father.

This is really no different to what happens today: double-minded about the Father's providence. Because of this double-mindedness, it creates the lukewarm mixture of the hot and cold toward God. Unsettled about what we think about God and how He will provide for us in the midst of circumstances or anytime really. The brass on the serpent is the lukewarm unsettled opinion about God. Notice that it's an opinion. It all starts in the heart. The people of Israel have seen the mighty hand of God move on their behalf, and they have seen some miraculous and powerful things take place right before their eyes. Was it a sin to doubt God? Was it a sin to have a negative opinion? Well, before there was an action, there was a thought. Jesus tells us in Matthew 12:34: "Out of the abundance of the heart, the mouth speaketh." The abundance there in Greek means "that what fills the heart." It is something that is meditated on.

Although we see Israel witnessing the Father's great power and providence, they begin to doubt and get unsettled in their opinion of God. They begin to see more of the negative things of being in the wilderness versus God with them. As they begin to see these things, they begin to feel the effects of being on this journey, and now the thoughts are becoming filled up with the lack of provision. Then the mouth spoke. That is the fruit of the heart being filled up so much it spills out of the mouth. It works for blessing and for cursing. The more you think on something, the more likely that it will come out of your mouth. It's not a sin to have a doubt. But it can become a sin if it's not dealt with. It's when something that is not true takes up residence in our minds and it stays there like a weed and gets watered, that creates issues.

> Finally, brethren, whatsoever things are true, whatsoever things *are* honest, whatsoever things *are* just, whatsoever things *are* pure, whatsoever things *are* lovely, whatsoever things *are* of good report; if *there be* any virtue, and if *there be* any praise, think on these things. (Philippians 4:8)

"And put it upon a *pole*." The word *pole* used here in the Hebrew is: נֵס (nace) which means "something lifted up, standard, signal, ensign, banner, signal pole." Remember part of the definition for dalet we studied previously? Lifted up and elevation!

> And as Moses lifted up the serpent in the wilderness, even so must the Son of man be lifted up: That whosoever believeth in him should not perish, but have eternal life. (John 3:14–15)

"When he *beheld* the serpent of brass, he lived." Looking at both John 3:14–15 and Numbers 21:9, whosoever believes in Him, Jesus, should not perish but have eternal life. When they beheld the serpent of brass, they lived.

Beheld, the English definition is "to gaze upon." Gaze means "to fix the eyes in a steady intent look often with eagerness or studious attention." Here in the Hebrew, it is the word: נָבַט (naw-vat') which means "to look, to regard, pay attention, to consider, have respect, regard with pleasure, favor or care." Looking into the ancient

Hebrew we have ⊗ ⊔ ⟍. This is a three-letter root word. From the right to the left: nun, bet (which in this case would be pronounced as a *V*) and tet. This word in the ancient Hebrew means "look, behold, regard, see, respect, *expect*."

> For he hath made him *to be* sin for us, who knew no sin; that we might be made the righteousness of God in him. (1 Corinthians 5:21)

When Jesus was on the cross, He literally took on all of the sin and *was made* sin. The brass serpent on the pole represented the sin of the people. The sin of the people was on the pole, and all they had to do was observe the serpent, and they would live. This is the picture of Christ! We should see our sin upon Him, for He was made sin that we would be made the righteousness of God and live.

When we come to His written Word, we are not just coming to a book for a nice leisure read. You could, but why do so when there's so much more to the Word and in the Word than that. This book has power, and that's because the Author breathed life into this Word and is a living thing. His Word is a person.

> All scripture is God-breathed and is useful for teaching, rebuking, correcting and training in righteousness. (2 Timothy 3:16 NIV)

> Holding forth the word of life. (Philippians 2:16)

If you don't know what the Word, or should I say Who the Word, is, then you won't know what to expect from reading it. If one knew that it was the power of God, one could expect to receive the power of God and see good fruit from it. If one just approached it as a regular reading book, there will be something done for sure but not to the degree that it could happen.

I like that word *expect* in the definition of the ancient Hebrew for *Nawvat*. That's how we should approach the Word of God: with expectation. We remember that Jesus, the Word, was crucified for our sakes and took on the form of sin so we can take on His righteousness. The Lord did something so that we could receive something. He didn't just do it so we could "feel good." He did it so that we would have eternal life and power. When Paul said, "Holding forth the Word of life," the "holding forth" in Greek is ἐπέχω (ep-ekh'-o) which means "to have, apply, to observe, attend to, give attention to." This is a compound word of ἐπί and ἔχω. ἐπί (ep-ee') which means "on, upon, at etc." ἔχω (ekh'-o) means "to have, to hold. Own, possess. To hold one's self to a thing, to lay hold of a thing, to adhere or cling to. To be closely joined to a person or a thing." You cannot possess, own, or hold anything you're not receiving. Behold Jesus in the Word as the Word and set an expectation of receiving from Him as you read the Word. As the Word is God-breathed, see Him breathe into you as you read His precious Word and receive the impartation of life, healing, and revelation. Possess the Word as your own. Have it take over your thoughts and make it your steady meditation.

> Now it came to pass, as they went, that he entered into a certain village: and a certain woman named Martha received him into her house. And she had a sister called Mary, which also sat at Jesus' feet, and heard his word. But Martha was cumbered about much serving, and came to him, and said, Lord, dost thou not care that my sister hath left me to serve alone? bid her therefore that she help me. And Jesus answered and said unto her, Martha, Martha, thou art careful and troubled about many things: But one thing is needful: and Mary hath chosen that good part, which shall not be taken away from her. (Luke 10:38–42)

Let's begin with Martha. We're talking about the expectation as we approach Jesus, the Word. Straightaway, we can see that Martha welcomed the Word into her house. It says that it was *Martha* who received him *into her house*. Then in verse 40, "But Martha was cumbered about much serving…"

Cumbered, in the English definition, means "to hinder or encumber by being in the way. To clutter up. Trouble. Harass." In the Greek, it is the word περισπάω (per-ee-spah'-o) which means "to draw around, to draw away, distract. To be driven about mentally, to be distracted. To be over-occupied, too busy, about a thing. To be distracted with cares. To be troubled, distressed." This word is not just about working on a specific task that requires thought space, but it is a word that speaks to being completely absorbed with something in anxiety. There are tasks that require our full mental attention, but there is no task that requires our absorption into the matter. This word is a compound of περί and σπάω. Beginning with the latter, σπάω (spah'-o), means "to draw. Draw out. As in draw one's sword." With just this word alone, if we were to use it in terms of thinking, it would be something that simply takes our attention for a brief moment in order to complete a task, like budgeting or something to that effect. However, there's a word attached to the front of it, so it changes it up a bit. This is the word περί (per-ee') which means "about, concerning, on account of, because of, around, near." Now, look at where this word comes from: the base of πέραν (per'-an), and it means "beyond, the other side." Placing this word in front of spaho, it tells us it's a total drawn away mind distracted by cares and overly busy in the mind with things.

Jesus pointed this out to her in verse 41: "Martha, Martha, thou art *careful* and *troubled* about *many things*."

Let's examine these words: careful, troubled, and many things.

Careful. In English, it means "marked by wary caution or prudence. Marked by *attentive concern* and solicitude. Marked by painstaking effort to avoid errors or omissions." Notice the "attentive concern." Attentive means "paying close attention to something." So in this case, she was paying close attention to other things. Remember the study with the fiery serpents. It was when they *beheld* the fiery serpent on the pole, not the fiery serpent on the ground, that they lived. Behold is paying close attention to… That is the plan of the enemy to distract one's mind from looking upon the cross and looking more attentively elsewhere. Rather than drawing from life, it's a drawing from dead things.

In the Greek, the word used here is μεριμνάω (mer-im-nah'-o) which means "to be anxious, to be troubled with cares. Caring or proving for." This word was used about nineteen times, and out of that, it was translated as "take thought" about eleven times. Therefore, this word is directly correlated with the thought life. *Merimnaho* comes from the word μέριμνα (mer'-im-nah) which means "care, anxiety." This comes from the word (through the idea of distraction) μερίζω (mer-id'-zo) which means "to divide, cut into pieces, split in factions." This is what distractions do. It cuts the mind up into pieces and decision-making becomes clouded, and emotions become rife. This is the same thing that we have been talking about from the start of this book. The distractions, drawing one away from reality in the mind, it's the same old tactic that was used in the garden of Eden that is still being used to this day. But thank God for Jesus! We have the victory!

I want to address this word *anxiety*. It gets tossed around a lot these days. Many people say they are feeling anxious about this or that. They also say that they have "bad anxiety." I have heard believers say this! It's one thing those in the world and sin would live with anxiety, but no child of God should ever live with anxiety! Look at this definition of anxiety: "fear or nervousness about what might happen. Apprehensive uneasiness or nervousness usually over an impending or *anticipated* ill."

I point your attention to the word *anticipated*. Anticipate means "to expect or look ahead to something. To give advance thought." The anxiety is caused by what is being looked at, whether the potential is real or not. It is all by what we are attentively looking at on the inside. What are we mediating on and thinking about most of the time? Is it the Father and His Word, or is it the latest news headlines, or is it the things that people are saying?

To have an anticipation of ill or bad is to not know what the Father wants for you. Which means you don't know the Word because inside the Word, it tells you all that He wants for you. Some people have even coped with anxiety thinking it's just the way of life. I tell you, friend, for the world, that may be true, but for a child of God, I tell you no, it is not true!

Look at where the word *anxiety* comes from: "apprehension caused by danger, misfortune, or error, uneasiness of mind respecting some uncertainty, a restless dread of some evil." It comes from the word anxious which comes from the Latin *anxius* meaning "solicitous, uneasy, troubled in mind" which comes from *anguere* which means "to choke, squeeze," figuratively "to torment, cause distress," and the very root word *angh* meaning "tight, painfully constricted, painful." What evil words used to define this word. This is not of God, and it is not for you. Second Timothy 1:7 says, "For God hath not given us the spirit of fear; but of power, and of love, and of a *sound mind.*" Look at what happens when cares like this enter into the heart and are left there to be mediated on. Jesus was talking about the parable of soils in this next passage, and He explained what the parable meant to His disciples:

> And these are they which are sown among
> thorns; such as hear the word, And the cares of
> this world, and the deceitfulness of riches, and the
> lusts of other things entering in, choke the word,
> and it becometh unfruitful. (Mark 4:18–19)

You can see how Martha received the Word into her house but cares, which is the same word that we just studied: μέριμνα (mer'-im-nah), entered in and choked the Word. Without getting ahead of ourselves here, Mary sat at the feet of Jesus and heard the Word. Martha had the same opportunity to give hospitality and hear the Word at the same time, but she was cumbered about with so many things on her mind she wasn't ready to hear the Word. As we said earlier, the Word is God-breathed. The word *choke* here in Mark 4:19 is: συμπνίγω (soom-pnee'-go), and it means "to choke utterly, to press round or throng one so as almost to suffocate him." This is a compound of σύν (soon) which means "with" and the word πνίγω (pnee'-go) which means "to choke, strangle," and this word comes from πνέω (pneh'-o) which means "to breathe, to blow."

When all the focus of our mind goes to other things and not drawing from His grace and from His Word and setting Him on our minds, we get concerned with the results of things. We draw from dead things, and that produces dead results or at least the expectation of it. This creates anxiety which chokes out the breath of the Word. In other words, it chokes out the revelation of the Word from within us! The power of the Word is in the revelation of Jesus Christ. Don't put up with anxiety another moment! Get in the Word, and get focused on His love for you today!

Troubled. In English, it means "concerned, worried." Concerned is "anxiety," and worried is "mentally troubled or concerned." The English words here are saying the same things as with careful. In the Greek, this is the word: θορυβάζω (toor-bad'-zo); it means "disturb, trouble, to be in troubled mind, disquieted." Disquieted means "unease." Now this Greek word has a root that is likened to the word θόρυβος (*thor'-oo-bos*), and it means "a noise, tumult, uproar," and its root is θροέω (*throeh'-o*) which means "to cry aloud, make a noise by outcry, to be troubled in mind, to be frightened, alarmed."

To me, with these defined, it seems that cares and anxieties are like loud noises in the mind to distract from the voice of reason, faith, and calm. When there's much going on in the mind, it can be hard to even hear yourself think. Cares are a thief and will rob everything from you if you let it. They must be dealt with, and they can only be dealt with the finished work of the cross!

We know that Martha was not just cumbered about with the serving of her guests, but there was a lot more going on the inside of her as Jesus pointed out in saying "many things." The serving was a normal thing when there were people coming over. This was not a one-time deal; it is cultural to give hospitality to guests. So the "many things" is not in relation to her serving. It was in relation to many other things. The word in the Greek that was used here is πολύς (*pol-oos*) which means "many, much, large." Martha had much going on in her mind distracting her from something that was far greater happening under her own roof.

Now, what Martha was doing was not incorrect. She was showing hospitality to her guests in her home, and that was the norm of the day. There's no fault in her doing this. Where the issue was, was in her thinking. Her mind was cluttered about and taken over with care and concern with the hospitality and, more likely, other things. Again, nothing wrong with the hospitality but when it takes over one's mind and disturbs one's peace, that is an issue for the person. That's what was going on with Martha. This is what goes on with many people today. Welcome Jesus in. Welcome the Word into the house, our temples. Then we get distracted with things of life and become overoccupied with these things until we are totally harassed in the mind. We then have the potential to take on the blaming of others for what's really happening only on the inside of ourselves and in our minds, just like Martha did in saying, "Lord, dost thou not care that my sister hath left me to serve alone? Bid her therefore that she helps me."

Let's look at what Mary was doing starting in verse 39: "Mary, which also sat at Jesus' feet, and heard his word." Jesus did not rebuke Mary for doing this when Martha called out Mary. Jesus said, "But one thing is needful: and Mary hath chosen that good part, which shall not be taken away from her."

The word *sat* in Greek here is παρακαθέζομαι (parakathezomai) which means "to make to sit down" and comes from a compound of: παρά (par-ah') meaning "from, of at, by, besides, near" and καθίζω (kathizō) which means "to make to sit down. To set, appoint, to confer a kingdom on one." This word comes from καθέζομαι (kathezomai) meaning "to sit down," and this word comes from a compound of κατά (kata) meaning "down from, throughout" and ἑδραῖος (hedraios) which means "sitting, sedentary. Firm, immovable, steadfast."

The very root of the Greek word for sit is immovable and steadfast. That is the benefits of sitting at the feet of the Word Himself; you will become steadfast and immoveable! Unlike the mind of wavering opinion wrapped up in cares and anxieties, the mind stayed on the Word is a mind that is settled and sure.

The name Martha means "she was rebellious." This is precisely what was going on in the wilderness. They rebelled in their minds toward God, and that's what happens when cares take over. In her very name is "she was rebellious." Now there's really good news here. The name Mary means "their rebellion." In Hebrew, it is: מִרְיָם (meer-yawm'), meaning "rebellion." Now the English definition of rebellion is "opposition to one in authority or dominance." Both sisters' names mean rebellious, but both had different outcomes. Just like those in the wilderness, they were all rebellious, but some had different outcomes. Any who would gaze upon the serpent on the pole would live and those who don't won't.

There may be moments of rebellion in our lives, but don't make a moment a monument where cares and concerns are concerned. Rather,

> *Looking* unto Jesus the author and finisher
> of *our faith*; who for the joy that was set before
> him endured the cross, despising the shame, and
> is set down at the right hand of the throne of
> God. (Hebrews 12:2)

If you started out in rebellion or fell into rebellion, it's simple to get right. The work is done through Christ! He took upon Himself all of the rebellion and set us right with God. Open His Word and approach it as you would approach Jesus Himself. Say before you even read, "I receive the very breath of God into my being and receive the revelation of Jesus Christ." Don't be cumbered about with other things, but sit at the feet of Jesus, and "that good part shall never be taken from you."

Looking ἀφοράω (af-or-ah'-o) means "to turn the eyes away from other things and fix them on something. To consider attentively."

One of our human problems is that we like to look at problems, attentively. Let's not look at the problem so attentively anymore. Let's look at Jesus more attentively. Keep your eyes on Him, and just like what happened in the wilderness for Israel, it will happen for you; you will live!

CHAPTER 6

The Author and the Finisher

I grew up in a Christian home going to church on Sundays and helping with kids, church, coffee shop, etc. I loved church, and I still do. My mom had a Bible that I absolutely loved. It was a big family Bible with the really thin pages that made that special sound when you turned the page. That was one of my favorite sounds in church: the turning pages of Bibles. Well, this was the Bible I would even pretend to preach with when I was a kid. It's a King James Bible, and I struggled with all of that Old English, so I would just pretend to know what it was saying. I think I was pretending for many years that I knew what the Bible was saying. It was when Jesus was revealed to me as *the* Word that my understanding and comprehension improved, and Faith came alive in me. Looking at Jesus as *the* Word changed my Bible studies and my life.

> Looking unto Jesus the author and finisher
> of *our* faith; who for the joy that was set before
> him endured the cross, despising the shame, and
> is set down at the right hand of the throne of
> God. (Hebrews 12:2)

The italicized words in the King James Version is an indication that the word was not there in the original language but was added for clarity. The word *our* is italicized. Therefore, it can be read as,

51

"Looking unto Jesus the author and finisher of faith..."_Not that there's anything wrong with "our faith," but I think it packs a real punch to see that Jesus is the author and finisher of faith, period!

> So then faith *cometh* by hearing, and hear-
> ing by the *word* of God. (<u>Romans 10:17</u>)

There's so much more to the Bible than just words and pages. It's more than a story, and it's more than instruction. Although the Bible is all of these things, it is more than that. The Word is a person. Now, that doesn't mean that I'm suggesting that we take our Bibles and make a shrine and worship it, but we should definitely place it in a high place in our lives and in our hearts.

Truly, we need preachers to preach and teachers to teach the Word of God. Surely, we need to read the Word, and we need to hear the Word. However, it is not by the mere listening that we get faith. The word *word* in this verse is the Greek word ῥῆμα (rhēma) which means, and I like how Thayers describes it, "that which is or has been uttered by the *living* voice." Preachers and teachers declaring the Word is a living voice but I believe there's deeper meaning to this word *rhema*.

When a person is engaged in the proclamation of the Word of God, they are yielding their voice to God's and to His will, mind and emotions. They are becoming God's voice. When the hearer hears this word, some people get full of faith and ready to take on lions while yet others may not experience anything at all. In other words, the immediate impact is varied among the hearers.

The same thing could be said for those who read the Word for themselves. So what would the difference be in the people whose faith was stirred up and those whose were not? It's in the rhema. Yes, the Word needs to be proclaimed, but it's the revelation of Jesus that stirs up faith. It's when the lights on the inside of a hearer get turned on. It's when the Holy Ghost speaks up on the inside and says, "Look!" Suddenly, that which could not be seen is seen and is known and as if it was under your nose the whole time!

The root for rhema is ῥέω (rheō), and this means "to pour forth, utter, speak, command." The "pouring forth" is through the speaking. Pour is "to cause to flow in a stream, to supply or produce freely or copiously, to give full expression to, to move with a continuous flow." So to get rhema, we should stay in a continuous flow of His Word, so hearing can produce faith! Notice the one definition "give full expression to." There's more going on with the proclamation of the Word than just someone making declarations. It's the avenue for the Spirit of God to move and point your eyes to Jesus, the Word! I pray your eyes are opening even now! To see! To see the one who loves you with all of His being!

Let's look back at Hebrews 12:2: "Looking unto Jesus the *author* and finisher of *our* faith…"

Author in the English definition is in part "one that originates or creates something: source." We get the word from the Latin *auctor* meaning "promoter, producer, father, progenitor; builder, founder; trustworthy writer, authority; doer; responsible person, teacher," literally "one who causes to grow." The root is *aug* which means "to increase."

The word for author used here in the Greek is ἀρχηγός (archēgos) which means "the chief leader, prince, one that takes the lead in anything and thus affords an example, a predecessor in a matter, pioneer, the author." This word is a compound of two words that I will list below in two separate paragraphs.

ἀρχή (archē) meaning "beginning, origin, the person or thing that commences, the first person or thing in a series, the leader, the first place, principality, rule, magistracy."

ἄγω (agō) which means "to lead, take with one."

Faith starts with the revelation of Jesus, is sustained by the revelation of Jesus, and increases through the revelation Jesus. Looking at these words to define the word, the author reveals there's really so much more here. Jesus is the Alpha and the Omega, the beginning and the end. Within the "author's" definition, we can see that He is everything in between the beginning and the end with the fact that He increases our faith! We're not supposed to just get one expression of Him but a continual expression of who He is! How do we do that? By the continual hearing of Him—the Word.

> We are bound to thank God always for you, brethren, as it is meet, because that your *faith groweth* exceedingly. (2 Thessalonians 1:3)

Faith is to be grown. It's not a one-time appointment. It's a continual feast. This is building a relationship with a person.

> And when the tempter came to him, he said, If thou be the Son of God, command that these stones be made bread. But he answered and said, It is written, Man shall not live by bread alone, *but by every word that proceedeth out of the mouth of God*. (Matthew 4:3–4)

> The just shall live by faith.(Habakkuk 2:4; Romans 1:17; Galatians 3:11; Hebrews 10:38)

We live according to how much we eat and what we eat. It's interesting to think that Jesus said that it was "man" that should not live by bread alone but by every word that comes from the mouth of God. Man covers all of humanity, not the sexual orientation. Yet when we look out at the world, we see a lot of people living and carrying on. Which then produces the question, what does it mean to live? To really live and have a full life, a fulfilling life, a satisfying life. It cannot be produced by things; they fade and get destroyed over time. It has to be something much greater and more profound than that which simply meets the eye. It's not that we don't have need of things, Jesus after all said "bread alone." There are things in the natural we need and that we want, but there's so much more available to us. So then if people are simply living by bread alone and not by every word that comes from the mouth of God, then they really aren't living.

Just as we need to eat a few meals throughout the day for natural sustenance and growth, we need that in the spirit as well. That comes by feeding on His Word. When we feed on His Word we are really feeding on the revelation of Jesus Christ, and that is where our growth is. Paul said in Hebrews 6:1: "Therefore, leaving the principles of the doctrine of Christ, let us go on unto perfection; not laying again the foundation of repentance from dead works, and of faith toward God."

When he said "perfection," that is the word for maturity. There's a growing up in the spirit that needs to take place for every believer.

> Our fathers did eat manna in the desert; as it is written, He gave them bread from heaven to eat. Then Jesus said unto them, Verily, verily, I say unto you, Moses gave you not that bread from heaven; but my Father giveth you the true bread from heaven. For the bread of God is he which cometh down from heaven, and giveth life unto the world. Then said they unto him, Lord, evermore give us this bread. And Jesus said unto them, I am the bread of life: he that cometh to me shall never hunger; and he that believeth on me shall never thirst. (John 6:31–35)

> Then said the LORD unto Moses, Behold, I will rain bread from heaven for you; and the people shall go out and gather a certain rate every day, that I may prove them, whether they will walk in my law, or no. (Exodus 16:4)

> Give us this day our daily bread. (Matthew 6:11)

There was a certain rate every day the people of Israel had to collect of the manna. Whatever they collected was only used for that one day except for the Sabbath. The day before the Sabbath, they collected twice the amount so they wouldn't have to collect on the Sabbath but still have food to eat on that day—daily sustenance on the bread from heaven. Jesus said that He is the True Bread from heaven, and when He was teaching His disciples how to pray, He said, "Give us this day our *daily* bread." This is a daily communion with the Lord: spending time in His Word, receiving the revelation of Jesus Christ, and growing our faith in His providence, grace, and love for us.

> And when the dew that lay was gone up, behold, upon the face of the wilderness *there* lay a small round thing, *as* small as the hoar frost on the ground. And when the children of Israel saw *it*, they said one to another, It *is* manna: for they wist not what it *was*. And Moses said unto them, This *is* the bread which the LORD hath given you to eat. (Exodus 16:14–15)

Manna in Hebrew is מָן (mān) which means, "What is it?" And this word comes from מָה (mâ), meaning "what, why, how, wherefore, etc." When people heard that Jesus was the Messiah, they all basically said, "mâ?" Or in other words, "What? How?"

> Philip findeth Nathanael, and saith unto him, We have found him, of whom Moses in the law, and the prophets, did write, Jesus of Nazareth, the son of Joseph. And Nathanael said unto him, *Can there any good thing come out of Nazareth?* Philip saith unto him, Come and see. (John 1:45–46)

In the ancient Hebrew, we find this word מָן (mān) to have these pictographs: ⟍ ᳚. The pictures from right to left are mem and nun. These combined mean "portion, what." "What comes from something else as one kind comes from the same." (Can anything good come out of Nazareth?) The root of this word, in the ancient Hebrew, is still spelled the same but holds a little more meaning to it: "firm; kind; sure." The mem, ᵚ, is a picture of water or other liquid such as blood. The nun, ᴎ, is a picture of a seed representing continuance. Combined, they mean "blood continues."

> And to Jesus the mediator of the new cove-
> nant, and to *the blood* of sprinkling, *that speaketh*
> better things than *that* of Abel. (<u>Hebrews 12:24</u>)

The Lord's blood continues! And it continues to speak righteousness, forgiveness, favor, love, kindness, faith, hope, surety, and so much more!

Let's look at the fourth verse of Exodus 16 again:

> I will *rain bread* from heaven for you.

The word *rain* literally means to rain down upon. The Hebrew word is מָטַר (māṭar), and do you recognize that first letter in the word? It is the letter mem that we just discussed. It represents water or other liquid such as blood. In this case, we are talking about rain, and it makes sense to start the word *rain* with the letter that represents water. Isn't the Hebrew language just so beautiful? What comes to mind with this rain, or water, is a pouring forth like we discovered earlier in the word ῥῆμα (rhēma) which again means "that which is or has been uttered by the living voice." Also, again, as a reminder, this word comes from ῥέω (rheō), and this means "*to pour forth*, utter, speak, command." He will pour forth bread, revelation of Jesus Christ, from heaven for you! The bread is the revelation of Jesus Christ. The scriptures are more than words; they are life! It is a revelation that only can come from heaven; it cannot be earthly created! There is far more than what meets the eye on our reading and in our hearing of God's precious and holy Word! He makes it rain revelation, and He does it for *you*!

The word *bread* is לֶחֶם (leḥem) which means "bread." It comes from לָחַם (lāḥam) which means "to fight, do battle, make war, to eat, use as food." Now we know that Jesus was born in Bethlehem.

Bethlehem in the Hebrew is בֵּית לֶחֶם (bêt leḥem) which means "house of bread." This is a compound of בַּיִת (bayit) meaning "house" and לֶחֶם (leḥem) "bread," if that wasn't cool enough.

> And she brought forth her firstborn son,
> and wrapped him in swaddling clothes, and laid
> him in a *manger*; because there was no room for
> them in the inn. (<u>Luke 2:7</u>)

That word *manger* in the Greek is φάτνη (phatnē) which means "a crib, a manger," and it comes from πατέομαι (pateomai) which means "to eat." The bread of life laid in a manger, meaning to eat!

Eat in Hebrew is אָכַל (aw-kal'). It starts with the letter א (aleph) which means strength. We derive our strength from our eating. This is both in the natural as well as in the spiritual. You will have to continually eat from the bread of heaven if you expect to grow spiritually.

> And the people shall go out and *gather a cer-*
> *tain rate* every day.

The word *gather* in Hebrew means "to gather, glean, collect, and to pick up." The words *a certain rate* is very intriguing. It is the word דָּבָר (daw-var) which means "speech, word, speaking, saying, utterance, business, occupation, acts, certain rate." Out of the 1,439 times this word was used, it was translated as "word" 807 times and as "thing" 231 times. The majority of its translation, 56 percent, was translated as "word." I think it's safe to say this word means word! So the people shall go out and glean, gather and collect His Word every day! Jesus, and the revelation of Him, is our daily bread, and in Him we live and not with bread alone.

> Looking unto Jesus the author and *finisher*
> of *our faith*. (<u>Hebrews 12:2</u>)

The word *finisher* in English means "to bring to an end, to bring to completion, to provide with a finish." Our faith starts with Jesus, grows in Jesus, and comes to completion, or full maturity, in Jesus. This word in the Greek is τελειωτής (tel-i-o-tace') which means "a perfector, one who has in his own person raised faith to its perfection and so set before us the highest example of faith." This word comes from τελειόω (tel-i-o'-o) which means "to make perfect, complete, consecrate, consummate." And this word comes from τέλειος (tel'-i-os) which means "brought to its end, finished, full grown, adult, of full age, mature."

The English word *finish* held the definition of "to bring to an end" in the late fourteenth century. It came from the Latin word *finis* meaning "a limit, an end, close, conclusion; an extremity, highest point; greatest degree." This word has unknown origins to etymologists but perhaps came from the word *figere* which means "to fasten, to fix," and that is where we get our word *fix* which from the fourteenth century held the definition of "set (one's eyes or mind) on something." Now in today's definition of fix, it means "to make firm, stable, or stationary. To give a permanent or final form to."

The word *faith* here in the Greek is πίστις (pis'-tis) which means "conviction of the truth of anything, belief, fidelity, faithfulness, the character of one who can be relied on, constancy in such profession." This comes from πείθω (pi'-tho) meaning "persuade, agree, be persuaded, be confident." Now, let's look at the Hebrew word for faith and compare it to the definition of fix.

אֵמוּן (ay-moon') meaning "faithfulness, trusting, trustworthiness." This word comes from אָמַן (aw-man') which means "to support, uphold, nourish, confirm, be faithful, to be established, be faithful, be carried, *make firm, stand firm*." See, when we fix our eyes on Jesus, when we see Him as the Word of God, our faith rises up on the inside of us as we receive the revelation of Him. This is what makes us stand firm and stable even on the times of what people would call uncertain times. I say what other people would call it because if you know Jesus, then there is no uncertain times for you. He has certain times for you! James 1:17 says there's no shadow of turning in Him. So stay in Him, and you won't have darkness, not even a shadow, but you will live in the light, and you will have certainty.

> And unto the angel of the church of the
> Laodiceans write; These things *saith the Amen,
> the faithful and true witness, the beginning of the
> creation of God.* (Revelation 3:14)

Amen here in the Greek is ἀμήν (am-ane') which means the same thing that it means in the Hebrew, *aw-man*, and that is "firm, faithful. At the end, so it is, so be it; may it be fulfilled." This actually comes from the Hebrew word אָמֵן (aw-man'). This is Jesus talking here in this verse. He called Himself the Amen!

The word *faith* comes out of this word *amen*! So it begins with the Amen, thus our faith is birthed, and it ends with the Amen at the conclusion of the matter.

> In the beginning was the Word, and the
> Word was with God, and the Word was God.
> The same was in the beginning with God. All
> things were made by him; and without him was
> not any thing made that was made. (John 1:1–3)

> Who is the image of the invisible God, the
> firstborn of every creature:
> For by him were all things created, that are
> in heaven, and that are in earth, visible and invis-
> ible, whether they be thrones, or dominions, or
> principalities, or powers: all things were created
> by him, and for him: And he is before all things,
> and by him all things consist. And He is the head
> of the body, the church: who is the beginning,
> the firstborn from the dead; that in all *things*
> He might have the preeminence. (Colossians
> 1:15–18)

> Declaring the end from the beginning, and
> from ancient times *the things* that are not *yet*

done, saying, My counsel shall stand, and I will
do all My pleasure. (Isaiah 46:10)

Jesus is that Word that was declared from the very beginning. The light that was and shined in the darkness when the earth was void and without form. This Light was released before the making of the sun, so this Light was *the* Light.

And God said, Let there be light: and there
was light. (Genesis 1:3)

The Hebrew word for "Let there be…" is the word הָיָה (haw-yaw) which means "to be, become, come to pass, exist, happen, fall out, come about, be established, to be done, to be finished." This word was used about seventy-five times and was translated as "was, come to pass, came, has been, were happened, become, pertained, better for thee." As opposed to the word *made* as in Genesis 1:7, "And God *made* the firmament…," and was used again when He made the stars, sun, and moon etc. The word *made* is עָשָׂה (aw-saw') which means "to do, fashion, accomplish, make, to produce." This word was used about 2,633 times and was translated as "do, make, wrought, deal, commit, offer, execute, keep, shew, prepare, work, do so, perform, get, dress, maker, maintain." In comparing the two, it's apparent that the Light was not created as the objects we see were (i.e., earth, plants, animals etc.) But it was released! The Light came from God and was God and was with God from everlasting! He released that Light that we might have life and life more abundantly!

Jesus is that Light, the Word of God, and the Word of God is Jesus. The Word of God is not separate from God that He would create His own Word from some other substance, but it is Him and was hence released from Him because that which already is cannot be created since it already exists but can only be released! Only that which is not must be created.

Then spake Jesus again unto them, saying,
I am the light of the world: he that followeth me

shall not walk in darkness, but shall have the light
of life. (John 8:12)

The Father declared the finished work, the Amen, from before the beginning of time. The Lamb was slain before the foundation of the world, and the Father looked and said, "Amen," then He began His work.

There's a story that goes with the Hebrew alphabet concerning the letter aleph. Everything in the Word of God is set there on purpose and with purpose. Certain words begin with certain letters for specific reasons, and certain words were placed in certain places for specific reasons. When we read Genesis 1:1,

> In the beginning God created the heaven
> and the earth.

הָאָרֶץ וְאֵת הַשָּׁמַיִם אֵת אֱלֹהִים בָּרָא בְּרֵאשִׁית
Beresheet Bara Elohim et h'shamim v'et h'eretz.

The first letter in the Torah is a beit. Well, if all words and letters are placed in proper order, why would the Torah begin with the letter beit rather than the aleph since that is the first letter? When God was placing the letters in order, the aleph had the opportunity to start God's Word, but in humility, the aleph stepped to the side and said, "Let Beit take the first place." It was then that God took the aleph and made it the number one letter of the Hebrew alphabet because of its willing sacrifice to put others before itself. Therefore, in lowliness and humility, the aleph was lifted up to another place of high honor. So beit then took its place as the starting letter of God's Word, and aleph took its place as the starting letter of all the letters.

The letter beit in the ancient Hebrew is in the shape of a spiral and looks like this: ⌂. This represents a tent, and the actual meaning of the letter is tent or house. This is the same letter that starts the word *son* in Hebrew which is the word: בֵּן (bane). This word comes from בָּנָה (bawnaw') which means "to build, rebuild, establish, cause to continue." The ancient Hebrew letters are ⌐ ⌂. The picture on the left is the nun. The definition in the ancient Hebrew is "son, one who continues the family line." The root of the word has the same letters with these meanings: "build, tent, panel, intelligence." The ⅁ means "house." The ⟍ is a sprouting seed representing continuity, thus when they are combined, it means "the continuing of the house."

Here, we see that the very beginning starts with the Son, the Amen. It is through Christ that Gods kingdom continues! Jesus is the wisdom of God, and look what is said in Proverbs 24:3: "Through wisdom is an house builded; and by understanding it is established." Also, John 8:35 says, "And the servant abideth not in the house for ever: *but* the Son abideth ever." All things point to Jesus, and by Him do all things exist and are sustained!

Going back to the brass serpent. Brass is a zinc and copper alloy. It's used on items for various reasons. One of the reasons is its durability and its ability to maintain its adhesion to an object regardless of bends and turns. It's highly conductive which is a reason why it is so widely used. When Jesus was on the cross and became sin for us, the fire of God came down and burned up all of the sin that He became. He dealt with sin once and for all on the cross. You could say the brass was a representation of the attraction of the fire, or the high-power electricity of God, to come down and burn up all the sin.

The brass covers another material, and it adds protection to the materials that are underneath. Jesus's blood covered all of our sin. He took every bit of the wrath of God upon Himself that we would not be touched by the wrath of God.

Zinc and copper are elements that are in our bodies and our bodies require if we want to be healthy. Low levels of zinc can increase risk of infections such as pneumonia. Zinc helps wound healing and the common cold. The list is quite lengthy with all the benefits zinc provides with protection from various diseases and illnesses. It includes the following: depression, diabetes, diaper rash, gingivitis, bad breath, cold sores, leprosy, stomach ulcers, bed sores, sickle cell disease, warts, ADHD, eye disease, and even acne.

Copper makes red blood cells, supports the immune system, forms a protein that helps make up bones and tissues, absorb iron into the body, and turns sugar into energy. Due do these qualities, a healthy amount of copper in the body can keep anemia and osteoporosis at bay.

I find it no coincidence that Moses used these materials for the serpent on the pole. These minerals provide health benefits; Jesus provides *life* and *healing* benefits! All of those complications that zinc and copper help defend Jesus bore it all! See your sickness and illness on the cross and live!

What's more is that there isn't even a lot of zinc and copper needed to benefit from them. It's just the same way with Jesus. You don't need to know everything; you just need to know enough. And that is Jesus became sin and sickness so that you could be righteous and whole. He died, rose again, and now lives as Lord.

I used to wonder about the medical community and the symbol they use including on ambulances. It's the serpent on the pole. For generations, they've used it, yet for generations, our governments have been opposing the Church of Christ and His ways. They removed prayer from schools, bible from schools, and in recent times have been removing the Ten Commandments from the front of court houses, to name a few. Many are opposing the "under God" portion of our pledge of allegiance. Now many schools don't have the pledge of allegiance, but that's for a whole other book for another time. It's been clear that the global governments want to remove as much of God from society as they can and set themselves up as god as much as they can. They like to give people money and other things so that the people would look to their government as their god and not to the one and only God. There's nothing wrong with a little assistance from government entities, but a full support system is not good.

So with all the removal of God from every corner possible, why is there no attack on the serpent on the pole with the medical community? The Lord showed my wife, Reena, the answer. For the same reason the governments want people to look to the governments as god (provider), the medical community wants people to look to them as god (healer). Now for clarity, I am not disparaging everyone in government and everyone in the medical community, but I am talking about the spirit that is behind all of these things.

Rather than looking to Jesus, who was the serpent on the pole, they want you to look at their serpent on the pole and think that you're going to get healed because they are here. Well, the fact of the matter is they heal none. They assist with the healing process, but they are no healers at all. There is only one Healer, and that is Jesus.

CHAPTER 7

Conclusion

The conclusion of the matter is Jesus *is* the Word. The Bible contains many stories that point to Jesus and many words that explain Jesus, but all in all, it *is* Jesus. This Word of God is so precious and so powerful it is like an iron first in a velvet glove. It contains power that no other writing on the planet contains and at the same time is wrapped in such love that transcends all understanding. I believe the Bible to contain the Spirit of Jesus from the very beginning and the very end. When we read its pages, we are breathing in His very nature and character. Yes, it renews our minds, but it builds our spirit man and heals all our flesh.

I believe when we have this revelation of the spirit and the Word coming together, it will take our study time to another level in Him. It will take our relationship with Him to a place we've only yet dreamed to be, and yet He will take it even farther than that.

Dear, reader, I don't know who is reading this or how many. But I do know there will be people in different places in their lives. I would like to personally address you in three different categories: 1) Believer in Christ, 2) Nonbeliever, 3) Believed and have gone elsewhere.

I pray for all three that you would all come to know Jesus and come to know Him more. That He would reveal Himself to you in greater ways that are material and tangible.

1) *My brother(s) and my sister(s).* With tears in my eyes, I am utterly grateful to be a part of this great body of Christ. I am thankful that you took the time to read the contents of this book. I pray that you fall in love with Jesus more and more. That you would experience all the depths of His love for you, His beloved bride. I know many of these things you probably already knew, but let it be a refreshing to you and strengthen you in your journey with Him. May your eyes be opened and your heart flooded with the revelation of Jesus Christ. May you prosper in all that you do. May God get all the glory through you.

2) *Dear friend.* You don't know Christ, but I pray that you will and that this book helped you to see Him. Countless numbers of people have already come to Him, and countless more are coming as the time draws closer for His coming for His church. There's no time to delay. You have delayed it enough as it is, and now is the time to thank God that you have made it this far, and ask Him into your life that you may go farther. Come join us and experience this love that nothing else on the planet can provide. All the things that you've been looking for can be found in Christ Jesus. Won't you take a minute and ask Him for help? God so loved *you* that He sent you His only begotten Son to die for *you*. Now, there's no wrong way to ask for help. A heart that is crying to God for help gets His attention. But if you find yourself searching for words try this: "Jesus, help me. Save me. Come into my heart and into my life, be my Lord."

There's a story in the Bible when Jesus was on the cross. He wasn't alone; there were two others at his side. One of them despised Jesus and blasphemed Him. The other called out to Him in a simple request: "Lord, remember me when thou comest into thy kingdom" (Luke 23:42).

Jesus did not reply to him that he was too late or that he did too great of sins or that he needs to get off the cross first and go do some good things. *No*, He replied, "Verily I say unto thee, To day shalt thou be with me in paradise" (Luke 23:43). Jesus also said in John 6:37, "All that the Father giveth me shall come to me; and him that cometh to me *I will in no wise cast out.*" He will not reject your request for not being eloquent enough or not having enough words or not even having the right works. He will accept you right here and right now!

If you just asked Him into your life for the first time, please let us know!! Welcome to the family! Go tell someone what the Lord has done for you! The next thing you need to do is find a bible-teaching, spirit-filled church to fellowship with like-minded people and get to know this Savior more!

3) *My brother(s) and sister(s)*. It's never too late to turn back and get back to things of God. You already know that He loves you, and you know the truths of the Word when it says that Jesus died for you. But did you know that you didn't go too far.

> Who shall separate us from the love of Christ? *shall* tribulation, or distress, or persecution, or famine, or nakedness, or peril, or sword? For I am persuaded, that neither death, nor life, nor angels, nor principalities, nor powers, nor things present, nor things to come, Nor height, nor depth, nor any other creature, shall be able to separate us from the love of God, which is in Christ Jesus our Lord. (Romans 8:35, 38–39)

Basically, *nothing* can separate you from His love! The only thing that really isn't mentioned in the list is ourselves. You are the only thing can separate you from the love of Christ. That is by flat out not wanting it and saying no to Him. But you can still say yes!

You can still turn it back around for God and get back into the things of Christ! There's time since you're reading this, but time is running out. The time is short, so the time should be now that you repent and come back to Jesus! Repent? Yes! Change your mind about how you are seeing God and let Him love you. The issue lies within yourself. Set your eyes upon Jesus and stop looking at yourself! Someone said, "But I don't want to." Well, I am talking to those who on the inside want to come back but feel they have gone too far or that the Lord won't take them back. For those who are still a hard no and have not thought of wanting Christ again, I pray that He will soften your heart and that you will see how much He truly loves and cares for you.

There are some who just ventured out into the world because they got bored with God or they simply were trying the taste of the world and in doing so got wrapped up in all the things the world has to offer. Friend, spit it out of your mouth and get back to Christ. Repentance is not hard! It just takes the first step. Get over the things of the world; sin took time, and it all started with the first step. Same thing here with getting back with Christ, the only difference is He has the power to accelerate you and get you back to where you should have been all along as though nothing had ever happened! Do it today! Come back to Him! He will not reject you; He will accept you and build you back up.

We serve a mighty God who adores you!

REFERENCES

All scripture references are taken from the King James Version

English definitions are from Webster's Dictionary and Oxford Dictionary

Ancient Hebrew Font is used with permission from Jeff A. Benner

ABOUT THE AUTHOR

Ken grew up in a Christian home. At about nine years old, he accepted Jesus as his Lord. Throughout his life, he has had various encounters with the Lord's presence. After having an intense spiritual experience and encountering the love of Jesus, his life has never been the same.

A student of the Greek, Hebrew, and ancient Hebrew, he seeks to reveal Jesus through the Word of God.